The Story of

GOLF

Dave Anderson

Foreword by **Jack Nicklaus**

WILLIAM MORROW AND COMPANY

New York

Permission for photographs is gratefully acknowledged: page 3—Golden Bear International; pages 13, 14 (bottom), 15, 16, 18, 21, 54, 73, 99, 100—United States Golf Association; pages 14 (top), 19, 27, 33, 39, 43, 44, 57, 59, 63, 75, 77, 78, 115—*Golf Digest*; pages 25, 28, 30, 51—Historic Golf Prints/The Frank Christian Collection; pages 37, 64, 67, 131, 133, 135, 143—AP/Wide World; pages 47, 137—Lester Nehamkin/*Golf Digest*; page 58—Rosanne Anderson; page 61—Jamie Squire/*Golf Digest*; pages 62, 70, 84, 89, 91, 92, 96, 105, 107, 111, 125, 127, 129, 132—Stephen Szurlej/*Golf Digest*; page 66—Gary Newkirk/*Golf Digest*; pages 69, 90, 109—Dom Furore/*Golf Digest*; page 80—Brett Avery/*Golf Digest*; page 81—Bill Fields/*Golf Digest*; page 121—NASA

Published by William Morrow and Company, Inc.
1350 Avenue of the Americas, New York, NY 10019
www.williammorrow.com

Printed in the United States of America.

10   9   8   7   6   5   4   3   2   1

Library of Congress Cataloging-in-Publication Data
Anderson, Dave.
The story of golf/Dave Anderson; foreword by Jack Nicklaus.
p.   cm.
Summary: Traces the development of the game of golf from its modern-day origins in fifteenth-century Scotland, highlighting key players, courses, and tournaments.
ISBN 0-688-15796-3
1. Golf—History—Juvenile literature.   [1. Golf—History.]
I. Title.   GV968.A53 1998   796.352—dc21   97-44097   CIP   AC

Foreword

AS LONG AS I CAN REMEMBER, I LOVED SPORTS— whether it was a team sport or an individual sport. I played and enjoyed baseball, football, basketball, and track. Then, when I was ten, my father introduced me to golf.

Although I enjoyed sports with my friends, I realized that golf was a sport that I could learn, practice, improve at, and enjoy by myself. I didn't need someone to throw the ball back to me or guard me. I liked that.

From the time I picked up a club, my summer days began and ended with golf. I would walk to the golf course each morning with my bag over my shoulder— through backyards and across fairways! I would hit balls, play 18 holes, hit more balls, and play another 18 holes. I would hit balls until dark or until my mother or father pulled me home by the ear.

The more I played golf, the more I wanted to learn about the game and its history. The more I learned, the more I wanted to play and excel at golf. If you are interested in golf, you can learn all about the great game in this terrific and informative book, *The Story of Golf*.

The beauty of golf, as you will discover, is that it is a game for a lifetime. I think you'll like that.

Enjoy *The Story of Golf*, and perhaps you will make golf your game for life!

Contents

part**One**

Scotland's Gift

TIGER WOODS PUMPED HIS RIGHT FIST AS HIS 12-FOOT birdie putt disappeared into the cup on Augusta National's 14th green. Winning the 1997 Masters was no longer the question. He now had a 12-stroke lead. When the twenty-one-year-old rookie pro maintained that victory margin with 4 finishing pars, he not only made golf history, but he also took it full circle from its roots as Scotland's gift to the world.

In golf's four major tournaments—the Masters, United States Open, British Open, and the Professional Golfers' Association (PGA) championship—nobody had dominated by that wide a margin since 1870 when Young Tom Morris, the nineteen-year-old son of legendary champion Old Tom Morris, won the British Open at Prestwick, Scotland, by 12 shots.

"I knew about the Masters record," Woods said, referring to his total of 270 strokes at Augusta National's par-72 course, one better than the 72-hole score set by Jack Nicklaus in 1965 and equaled by Raymond Floyd in 1976. "But I didn't know about nobody winning a major by twelve shots since 1870. That's a long time."

In that time, golf had grown from a simple game played in Scotland with fragile wooden clubs and leather-covered balls into a billion-dollar industry with more than fifty million variously skilled men, women, boys, and girls at nearly thirty thousand public, private, and resort courses; dozens of wealthy world-touring professionals; and hundreds of golf-equipment and golf-related companies selling exotic high-tech clubs, balls, and apparel.

But golf really wasn't any different for Eldrick ("Tiger") Woods than it was for Young Tom Morris in Scotland more than a century ago—tee up a ball, hit it with a golf club, find it, then keep hitting it, finding it, and hitting it until it dropped into the cup some 500 or 400 or 300 or 150 yards away.

Unlike other sports, in which the most points or runs or goals determine a winner, a golf winner makes the fewest strokes. In medal, or stroke, play over 18 holes, a 68 is better than a 69. In hole-by-hole, or match, play, a golf winner has won more holes than there are holes remaining to play; if a golfer is 3 holes ahead with only 2 to play, for example, that golfer has won, 3 and 2.

Par is the accepted score for a hole, depending on its length—par 3, par 4, par 5. Birdie is a score that is 1 under par on a hole; eagle is 2 under par; double-eagle is 3 under par. Bogey is 1 over par on a hole; double-bogey is 2 over par; triple-bogey is 3 over par, etc.

Another element of golf that doesn't exist in most other sports is the handicap system. If a golfer's average score on a par-72 course is 72, that person is known as a scratch golfer. If a person has a 4 handicap, that golfer would usually shoot 76; a person with a 14 handicap would usually shoot 86. Theoretically, the handicap system allows golfers of various abilities to play one another even. The 4 handicap golfer would give the 14 handicap golfer a stroke on the 10 most difficult holes on that particular course in match play, or 10 strokes overall in stroke play.

Although the clubs known as woods are mostly made of metal now, a driver is considered a 1-wood, a brassie a 2-wood, a spoon a 3-wood, etc. The irons, from 1 to 9 to pitching wedge, have various degrees of loft to provide trajectory. The sand-wedge is used out of bunkers, sometimes off grass. On the green, a golfer uses a putter to putt the ball into the hole.

The Romans had used sticks and feather-stuffed leather balls to play a game called *paganica*, which the French, Dutch, and English adopted in various forms. The Dutch argue that they invented golf, but the first written mention of golf is found in an Act of Parliament in Scotland in 1457. The government had tried to ban the game because its popularity was interfering with practicing archery, a citizen's primary military duty in the wars of that medieval era. But the new law had little effect.

Two later Scottish Parliaments also tried, unsuccessfully, to outlaw golf. King James IV and King James V both became avid golfers, and Mary, Queen of Scots, played at St. Andrews before her death in 1587.

Although some historians argue that golf was played at Royal Blackheath in London as early as 1608, the Honourable Company of Edinburgh Golfers is considered the first organized golf club. Formed in 1744 and now based at the Muirfield Golf Club near Edinburgh, it also issued the original thirteen Rules of Golf, adopted almost word for word by the Royal and Ancient Golf Club of St. Andrews when it was formed in 1754. Known by its initials, the R and A has its headquarters in what is considered to be golf's ancestral home, the gray stone clubhouse overlooking the 1st tee and the 18th green of the Old Course at St. Andrews on Scotland's eastern coast.

But why are there 18 holes on a golf course? Why not another number?

According to the *Encyclopaedia of Golf*, St. Andrews originally was a 12-hole course, with the 11th hole at the far end. When golfers got there, they had to play back again to the same greens and same holes in the greens (apart from the 11th and 18th, which are at opposite ends of the course), in the reverse direction, making a normal round 22 holes. In 1764, however, the first 4 holes were converted into 2 and, as the same thing happened on the way in, the round became 18 holes.

Throughout the world, a joint committee of the United States Golf Association (USGA) and the R and A governs the Rules of Golf, which depend on a code of honor unlike that of any other sport. Golfers have been known to call penalties on themselves when their ball moved slightly, even though nobody else saw it move. Golf's basic rule now is the same as it was in the Articles and Code of Playing Golf, St. Andrews, 1754: "After driving off, the player must play the ball as it lay and not interfere with his opponent's ball—the ball must not be touched with anything but a club until it is holed out."

Those early golfers used primitive clubs with wooden shafts, some with wooden heads, others with iron facings, to hit feather-stuffed leather balls across unkept terrain to unmowed greens. Herds of grazing sheep were often that era's greenkeepers. But that didn't deter women, in their long skirts, from the game. By 1810, the Musselburgh (Scotland) Club offered a prize for a women's competition.

During the nineteenth century, Allan Robertson, who operated St. Andrews's golf shop, was considered Scotland's best player. To determine his successor following his death in 1859, golf's oldest tournament, the British Open (or the Open Championship, to use its official title) was held for the first time in 1860.

In three rounds over Prestwick's 12-hole course, Willie Park, a Scottish pro, won with a 36-hole score of 174. Old Tom Morris would win four of the next seven titles with the new leather ball filled with gutta-percha, a rubberlike substance from Malaysian trees. Young Tom Morris won the following four Opens, his first at age seventeen, but he died at age twenty-four, apparently of a broken heart soon after the sudden death of both his wife and his newborn baby. As good as Robertson and Old Tom Morris had been, Young Tom, who set the Old Course record with a 77, was considered a phenom, the Tiger Woods of his time.

"I could cope wi' Allan myself," Old Tom once said in his Scottish burr, "but never wi' Tommy."

Old Tom Morris would also be involved indirectly with John Reid, who emerged as the Father of American Golf. Growing up in Dunfermline, Scotland, Reid had watched golf but never played. Upon emigrating to New York City, where he was an ironworks executive, he remembered golf's growing popularity in Scotland. When

Old Tom Morris and Young Tom Morris

Old Tom Morris, his white beard similar to that of Santa Claus, sits with more than two dozen of the early golfers he inspired.

his friend, Robert Lockhart, mentioned he was returning to Scotland for the Christmas holidays, Reid asked him to purchase a set of clubs and some balls.

Lockhart visited Old Tom Morris's shop in St. Andrews and returned with two dozen gutta-percha balls and a set of clubs—three woods (driver, brassie, spoon) and three irons (cleek, sand-iron, putter). He arranged for the box of clubs and balls to be shipped to his New York City home.

On his return, Lockhart took the box to Reid's home. When the weather turned out to be relatively warm and sunny on February 22, 1888, Reid, who lived in Yonkers just north of the New York City border, took his new clubs to his cow pasture, where he met some friends.

Over 3 holes each about 100

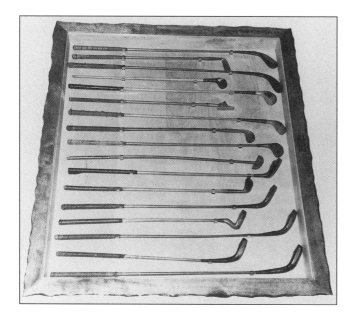

In the 1800s, golf clubs were shaped differently.

yards long, with cups scooped out of the ground with one of the irons, Reid and John B. Upham played the United States' first golf match that afternoon. No score was kept, but fifteen years after North America's first golf club, Royal Montreal in Canada, had been founded, the game had arrived in the United States. Several of Reid's friends soon ordered clubs and balls from Scotland. Later that year, they moved to a 6-hole course laid out in another cow pasture. And on November 14, 1888, at a dinner in Reid's home, the United States' first golf club, St. Andrew's, was officially founded. Reid was unanimously elected president.

With a tent serving as the St. Andrew's clubhouse, the membership quickly rose to thirteen, and in 1892 the club moved to a larger tract of land. After a 6-hole round there, the members gathered for sandwiches and drinks in the shade of an old apple tree, prompting their nickname, the Apple Tree Gang, that would live in golf history.

Members of the Apple Tree Gang at St. Andrew's

Charles Blair
Macdonald

By then, another disciple of Old Tom Morris, husky Charles Blair Macdonald, was spreading golf's gospel in Chicago. Two decades earlier, Macdonald had attended St. Andrews University in Scotland, where his grandfather took him to Old Tom's shop and bought him a set of clubs. He soon was good enough to play with Young Tom Morris before the phenom's death. With his passion for the game, he built the United States' first 18-hole course, the Chicago Golf Club in Wheaton, Illinois, which opened in 1895. He also developed into the first noteworthy American-born golfer and, indirectly, provoked the founding of the USGA, which now conducts thirteen national championship tournaments.

When the Newport (Rhode Island) Country Club invited United States golfers to gather in 1894 at its 9-hole course for separate 36-hole "national" championships for amateurs and pros, Macdonald's score of 89 opened a 4-stroke lead in the amateur event. But the next day W. G. Lawrence won by a stroke when Macdonald's 100 included a 2-shot penalty for a ball snuggled against a stone wall.

Macdonald, whose ego was larger than he was, complained about the penalty and argued that the championship should not be at medal (stroke by stroke) play but at match play, which is scored on a hole-by-hole basis. When he later lost a similar "national" tournament—this time at match play—at St. Andrew's near New York City, he growled that it hadn't been an official national championship because only an official national association of golf clubs could sanction an official national championship. Fearing bad feelings between the eastern and midwestern golfers, a Newport member, Theodore Havemeyer, suggested that representatives of five clubs—Newport; Shinnecock Hills in Southampton, New York; St. Andrew's; Chicago; and The Country Club in Brookline, Massachusetts—meet on December 22, 1894, to form a national governing body. Havemeyer was elected president and Macdonald vice-president of what is now the USGA.

In 1895 at Newport, Macdonald won the first official U.S. Amateur in a 36-hole final against Charles Sands, 12 and 11, and Horace Rawlins, a Shinnecock Hills assistant pro from England, won the first official U.S. Open with a 36-hole total of 173, 2 ahead of Willie Dunn, a Scot who was Rawlins's boss at Shinnecock Hills.

Even then, golf was a game for everybody, not just wealthy men who could afford it. That same year, Mrs. C. S. Brown won the first U.S. Women's Amateur title with an 18-hole score of 132 at the Meadow Brook Club in Hempstead, New York, and the United States' first public course was built at Van Cortlandt Park in the Bronx, a borough of New York City.

But the game was changing. In 1898, the U.S. Open expanded to 72 holes, and Coburn Haskell, a Cleveland golfer, developed a rubber-cored ball. It soon would replace the gutta-percha as the ball of choice for the same simple reason that today's golfers buy whatever new ball is on the market: It soared several yards farther.

Golf in America was also being popularized by the Scottish and English professionals. Many were hired as teaching pros at more than a thousand courses, mostly in the East and Midwest, as Harry Vardon, the husky Englishman who had already won three of his record six British Open titles, won the 1900 U.S. Open at the Chicago Golf

Club. The next year, Willie Anderson, a transplanted Scot, won his first of a record-sharing four U.S. Open championships in a span of only five years. Then in 1911, Johnny McDermott, a nineteen-year-old pro from Atlantic City, New Jersey, became the first American-born golfer to win the U.S. Open.

By then, Walter Travis, who was born in Australia but learned to play in the New York area, had won three U.S. Amateurs (as well as the 1904 British Amateur), and Jerry Travers, who grew up in the New York area, was on the way to winning four U.S. Amateurs, a total that would be surpassed eventually only by Bobby Jones's five.

Harry Vardon

But the most compelling moment in the United States' early golf history occurred in the 1913 U.S. Open when twenty-year-old Francis Ouimet, the Massachusetts Amateur champion who lived across the street from The Country Club outside Boston, calmly forced an 18-hole playoff with two Englishmen, the legendary Harry Vardon and long-hitting Ted Ray, who had won the 1912 British Open. Each shot 304, with Ouimet sinking a 20-foot birdie putt on the 17th hole of the final round and a 5-footer on the 18th.

Francis Ouimet and his older brother, Wilfred, had built a 3-hole course in their backyard with sunken tomato cans for cups. Their first club had been given to Wilfred by a member of The Country Club. They later obtained a mashie (now a 5-iron) and a brassie (now a 2-wood) in trades for the dozens of balls they had found.

The rainy morning of the playoff, Ouimet was walking to the 1st tee from the practice range when the two-time U.S. Open champion, Johnny McDermott, approached him. "You're hitting the ball well," McDermott said. "Now go out and pay no attention whatsoever to Vardon and Ray. Play your own game."

Ouimet did just that. Each shot a 2-over-par 38 on the front 9; then Ouimet took a 1-stroke lead at the 10th. On the 12th, his par provided a 2-stroke lead. Vardon birdied the 13th, but Ray soon was out of it after a double-bogey at the 15th and a bogey at the 16th. On the 17th, a dogleg left, Vardon hooked his tee shot into tangled rough. Ouimet was in the fairway. Vardon bogied; Ouimet birdied for a 3-shot lead. On the 18th, with the Boston gallery of thirty-five hundred cheering the United States' first golf icon and their own hometown hero, Ouimet calmly finished with a par for a 72, 5 shots ahead of Vardon, 6 ahead of Ray.

The tall amateur with the Bostonian accent had not only won the U.S. Open, but he had also defeated Great Britain's two premier golfers.

"I am as much surprised and

Francis Ouimet

pleased as anyone here," he said upon being presented with the Havemeyer Trophy. "Naturally it was always my hope to win out. I simply tried my best to keep this cup from going to our friends across the water. I am very glad to have been the agency for keeping the cup in America."

More than any other United States golfer in that era long before television, Francis Ouimet had put golf on page one of the nation's newspapers. Scotland's gift was now America's treasure.

H E WAS KNOWN AS SIR WALTER, OR THE HAIG, AND he was America's first golf ambassador.

In the 1913 U.S. Open won by Francis Ouimet in a theatrical play-off, Walter Hagen, a happy and husky twenty-one-year-old pro out of Rochester, New York, was a forgotten fourth-place finisher. But he would never be forgotten again. He would win the 1914 and 1919 U.S. Opens and, from 1921 to 1929, five PGA Championships and four British Opens. He would win acceptance for touring pros in snobbish clubhouses all over the world. And he would win fans of golf with his lively lifestyle.

Walter Hagen swung as stylishly as he dressed.

The son of a blacksmith, Hagen was a caddie at the Country Club of Rochester at age nine, earning ten cents for 18 holes, with a five-cent tip. After quitting school at twelve, he had part-time jobs as a piano finisher, taxidermist, apprentice to a mandolin maker, and a garage mechanic while also working in the Country Club of Rochester's pro shop. In 1913, at twenty, he was the club pro. In 1919, at twenty-six, having won the U.S. Open twice, he was already a legend.

"Never hurry and don't worry," he liked to say. "You're here for just a short visit, so don't forget to stop and smell the flowers."

He smelled the flowers and knew how to have fun. He wore silk shirts, soft tweed slacks, and two-tone shoes. He partied into the wee hours, but he often was seen dumping his scotch into flowerpots rather than drinking it. Other times, he was really drinking iced tea. He once arrived at a course in a tuxedo. After nights on the town, he often played the 1st hole in patent-leather shoes, then changed into his golf spikes, which his caddie-chauffeur-valet, Spec Hammond, had been wearing for him.

"That man," Hammond growled quietly, "ruined my feet."

But that man also understood, perhaps better than anyone, how to cope with the frustrations of golf that plague not only duffers but also the great champions.

"It's normal to make three or four bad shots a round," Hagen said. "When you make a bad shot, forget about it."

If Francis Ouimet put golf on page one, Walter Hagen put it on a pedestal. At the 1913 U.S. Open, golf pros were not allowed inside The Country Club's clubhouse. In that era, snooty club members looked down on the transplanted Scottish and English pros as well as on the young American-born pros. But at the 1914 U.S. Open at Midlothian outside Chicago, Hagen not only won the tournament but also led the pros into the clubhouse's locker room. He was just as brash on the golf course.

On the first tee of a tournament, he would look around and say,

"Well, who's going to be second?"

To the dismay of his opponents, he backed up his brashness as no other golfer ever has.

On the final green of the 1919 U.S. Open at Brae Burn outside Boston, he needed an 8-foot putt to force an 18-hole playoff with Mike Brady, who had already finished.

"Get Mike out here," Hagen yelled. "I want him to see this."

As Brady watched, Hagen holed his putt. That evening, Hagen was having a good time well past midnight when he was reminded that Brady had gone to bed early.

"He might be in bed," Hagen said, "but he's not sleeping."

Hagen won the playoff, then returned to Oakland Hills outside Detroit and resigned as the club pro.

"Here's my replacement," he said. "Mike Brady."

Before the 1920 Open at Inverness in Toledo, Ohio, eighteen-year-old Gene Sarazen, who would be one of Hagen's rivals, was sitting in the locker room.

"Two heroes of mine, Harry Vardon and Ted Ray, had already come in," Sarazen recalled. "Then Walter marched in, head high, looking like he was the sultan of someplace or other. That was Walter Hagen for you. He acted like he was the whole show all the time."

Sarazen remembered another Hagen moment, before the 1921 U.S. Open at the Columbia Country Club in Chevy Chase, Maryland, outside Washington, D.C.

"Walter was in the locker room shaving while President Warren Harding waited for him on the first tee," Sarazen said. "There was Walter, without a care in the world, keeping the President of the United States waiting."

The next year, 1922, Gene Sarazen surfaced as a golf phenom at a level many people were unaware of until Sarazen was asked in 1996 what he thought of then twenty-year-old Tiger Woods, still a Stanford University sophomore.

"Well," Sarazen said gently, "when I was twenty, I won the U.S. Open and the PGA."

Born Eugenio Saraceni in Harrison, New York, near New York City, he was an eleven-year-old caddie when he heard about Francis Ouimet's victory. At sixteen, he left school to help his father, a carpenter, support their family during World War I.

"I helped my father build an army barracks," he once said. "That's how I learned to hit the ball. I had to hit those nails on the head, or they would bend."

At eighteen, Sarazen contracted tuberculosis, a lung disease that at the time often confined its victims to mountain-area sanitariums, where they could breathe cleaner air.

"The doctors saved me," he said, "with an operation never before tried in the United States. They cut through my ribs and inserted a hose to clear my lungs."

Even though Sarazen had played in two U.S. Opens as a teenager, he was virtually unknown when he arrived at Skokie outside Chicago before the 1922 U.S. Open, the first to charge admission. Tickets were one dollar each. Two days before the tournament began, he noticed Ouimet, Jim Barnes (the defending U.S. Open champion, who had also won the first two PGA titles in 1916 and 1919) and Chick Evans (the 1916 U.S. Open champion) about to tee off in a practice round.

"Do you mind if I make the fourth?" Sarazen asked.

"I wouldn't like that," Barnes replied stiffly.

By week's end, Sarazen had dethroned Barnes, edging Atlanta's phenom, twenty-year-old Bobby Jones, by one stroke. Later that year, at Oakmont outside Pittsburgh, Sarazen captured his first of three PGA titles. In 1932, he produced another double, winning the U.S. Open at Fresh Meadow near New York City and the British Open at Prince's in England.

During the second Masters tournament, in 1935, he would produce what lives as golf's single most memorable shot.

Sarazen had hit his tee shot on the par-5 15th hole in the final round when he heard a roar from the 18th green. Craig Wood had finished with a 72-hole score of 282, an apparent winner. Of those golfers still on the course, only Sarazen had a chance, but he would need to birdie 3 of the last 4 holes to tie. Now, peering beyond the pond to the flagstick about 220 yards away, Sarazen, who was playing with Walter Hagen, was wondering what club to hit.

"Hurry up," Hagen said. "I've got a date tonight."

Sarazen considered using his 3-wood, but chose his 4-wood. Toeing it in slightly, he swung. His ball soared high and straight, landed on the green, and rolled into the cup for a double-eagle 2, a rare 3-under-par score that was the equivalent of the 3 birdies he

Gene Sarazen put the Masters on the golf map with his double-eagle 2 at the 15th hole in 1935.

had needed to force a 36-hole playoff the next day. He parred each of the last 3 holes, then routed Wood, 144-149, in their playoff.

In his travels all over the world for more than sixty years after that 4-wood shot, Sarazen would always be identified with it.

He also would be identified by his knickers, or plus fours, that he wore into his nineties when hitting the ceremonial tee shot on Augusta National's first hole at the Masters.

"Everybody wore them when I was young, and I never stopped," he said. "They're comfortable. I get tangled up in long pants, but nobody makes long woolen socks these days."

In that era before television, no cameras were at the 15th hole to record his double-eagle 2 there. Not many spectators saw it.

"There weren't more than two dozen people standing behind the green," Sarazen often recalled. "One of them was Bobby Jones."

No one could have had a more respected witness to a memorable shot. Bobby Jones, with his Grand Slam in 1930 and his founding of the Masters, had surpassed both Sarazen and Hagen in popularity. He would endure as a golf legend until his death in 1971.

Over a span of seven years, Jones, an amateur who was an Atlanta attorney, won the U.S. Open four times, the British Open three times, the U.S. Amateur five times, and the British Amateur once.

His only British Amateur victory occurred in 1930, when he swept all four of the major championships for his celebrated Grand Slam, then suddenly retired from serious competition at age twenty-eight.

Born on March 17, 1902, in Atlanta, Jones was a sickly child but nonetheless developed into a golf prodigy. When he was five, to escape Atlanta's steamy summer heat, his father moved the family to a boarding house near the East Lake Country Club at the end of the city's trolley line. Soon little Bobby was swinging a cut-down iron and following the East Lake pro, Stewart Maiden, around the course. He had found the game that would make him famous wherever golf was played.

At nine, he won the Atlanta Athletic Club's junior title, defeating a sixteen-year-old. At thirteen, he won a men's invitational tournament in Birmingham, Alabama. At fourteen, after winning the East Lake Invitational and the Georgia Amateur, he entered the 1916 U.S. Amateur at Merion outside Philadelphia. In his first pair of long pants and wearing golf spikes on brown shoes, he won two matches before losing in the quarterfinals, 5 and 3, to Robert Gardner, the defending champion.

At age fourteen,
Bobby Jones
competed in
his first
U.S. Amateur.

Bobby Jones

When the U.S. Amateur resumed after World War I, Jones returned, but he didn't win that title until 1924, at Merion. The year before, at age twenty-one, he had won his first U.S. Open, at Inwood in the New York inlets near what is now the John F. Kennedy International Airport.

By then, Jones had entered Emory University Law School after having earned two college degrees—one at age eighteen in mechanical engineering at Georgia Tech after only three years, the other at age twenty-one in English at Harvard after only three semesters.

Jones also had learned to control the temper that threatened to betray his skill. In the 1921 British Open at St. Andrews, he had torn up his scorecard after the third round, an act that he later called "the most inglorious feature" of his career.

Each year, beginning in 1923 through his Grand Slam in 1930, Jones won at least one of the four major titles of that era—the U.S. Open, the British Open, the U.S. Amateur, and the British Amateur. In those years, long before virtually all of the world's best golfers were on the PGA Tour, several amateur golfers were considered to be as skilled as many of the pros.

But of all the pros or amateurs in that era, Jones was the most skilled of all, and arguably the most skilled of any era.

As good as Hagen and Sarazen were, neither ever won a U.S. Open or a British Open that Jones had also entered. In addition to his four U.S. Open titles, Jones lost two 36-hole U.S. Open playoffs— to Johnny Farrell (by 1 stroke) in 1928 at Olympia Fields outside Chicago, and to Willie Macfarlane (by 1 stroke) in 1925 at the Worcester (Massachusetts) Country Club after he had called a 1-stroke penalty on himself in the first round.

In the rough, Jones's practice swing grazed the grass. He noticed that his ball had moved. Only slightly, but it moved. Nobody else saw it move, but he had. Under the Rules of Golf, he knew that he had incurred a penalty stroke. He called it on himself, adding an extra stroke to his score on that hole. As it turned out, that stroke made the difference between his winning the U.S. Open outright and being in the playoff he lost.

When Jones was praised for his honesty, he said, "You might as well praise a man for not robbing a bank."

Unlike other sports, where competitors depend on the judgment of umpires or referees, in golf it's up to the players to call penalties in a situation such as Jones's noticing that his ball had moved. Honor and honesty are an integral part of golf conduct. That penalty stroke in the 1925 U.S. Open is one reason that the USGA's revered sportsmanship award is named for Bobby Jones.

He is remembered best, of course, for his Grand Slam in 1930, a feat that in a 1997 poll of golf officials and golf writers would be voted the game's most memorable moment and a feat that, he later acknowledged, he had planned with "precisely this end" in mind.

Early that summer, he won the British Amateur at St. Andrews, rallying twice in earlier rounds and then routing Roger Wethered,

7 and 6, in the scheduled 36-hole final. Three weeks later, at Hoylake in England, he won the British Open, 2 strokes ahead of Leo Diegel and Macdonald Smith. He knew he had played erratically; yet he had won both championships.

"I think this is what I learned to do best of all," he said years later. "The most acute, and yet the most satisfying, recollections I have are of the tournaments won by triumphs over my own mistakes and by crucial strokes played with imagination and precision when anything ordinary would not have succeeded."

Four early Masters on the first tee— Tommy Armour, Walter Hagen, Gene Sarazen, and Bobby Jones

Returning for the U.S. Open at Interlachen in Minneapolis, he won by 2 over Macdonald Smith, then breezed through the U.S. Amateur at Merion, disposing of Gene Homans, 8 and 7, in the final. The moment his winning putt disappeared, he was surrounded by four dozen Marines in dress-blue uniforms, who ushered him through the stampeding gallery of eighteen thousand to the clubhouse.

"I waited for him with his clubs," his caddie, Howard Rexford, later recalled. "After a while, he came out, thanked me, and put some money in my hand. I didn't even look at it. He took his clubs. I went outside and hid and looked. There were fifteen ten-dollar bills—one hundred fifty dollars. In the Depression, that was a real fortune."

After announcing his retirement from competition, Jones mostly concentrated on his law practice, but he went to Hollywood to do twelve instructional golf films for Warner Brothers. He also designed Spalding golf clubs. In 1933, he founded the Augusta National Golf Club and codesigned its course with architect Alister MacKenzie.

In 1934, he organized the Masters that his legend still dominates, the tournament that many golfers now consider to be the world's most prestigious, the tournament that would be his legacy.

HITTING A GOLF BALL SOLIDLY WITH A GOLF CLUB IS arguably the most difficult task in sports. Because the ball is so small, it sometimes is snuggled in thick grass or sand bunkers. The clubs are so variable. And a golfer's swing is so elusive, if it's off line by even a millimeter, the ball will go this way or that, or sometimes nowhere.

But in winning a record eleven consecutive PGA Tour events in 1945, Byron Nelson's swing resembled a machine.

"The mechanics of my swing were such that no thought was required," the tall Texan with the huge hands once said. "It's like eating. You don't think to feed yourself. All my concentration was on the scoring, not the swing, so I'll never know what caused it. The main thing I worried about was my tempo. I was afraid of losing it, but I couldn't lose it."

Not that year. Not even when his streak had become a burden.

As he won nine straight tournaments, including the PGA Championship (golf's only major during the summer when World War II ended), the same headline greeted him in the local newspaper wherever he went: CAN NELSON WIN AGAIN? He was weary from the expectations that surrounded his every swing, his every putt. The morning of the first round of his next tournament, the Tam O'Shanter outside Chicago, he turned to his wife, Louise.

"I hope I blow up," he told her.

When he returned several hours later, Louise asked, "Well, did you blow up?"

"Yeah," he said. "I shot 66."

The next day, the golfer known as Lord Byron shot 68, followed by another 68 and a 67 for 269, a total of 19 under par, and his tenth consecutive victory. The next weekend, he won the Canadian Open at Thornhill in Toronto, his record eleventh straight. Two weeks later, his streak ended. He tied for fourth at the Memphis (Tennessee) Invitational won by Fred Haas, Jr.

In winning eleven consecutive tournaments in 1945, Byron Nelson seemed to make all his putts.

His first eight victories in the streak were at the Miami Four-Ball (with Jug McSpaden); Charlotte, Greensboro, Durham (all in North Carolina); Atlanta; Montreal; Philadelphia; and the Victory Open (a wartime substitute for the U.S. Open) at Calumet Country Club outside Chicago. With three victories before the streak and four more after it, Nelson won a record eighteen of his thirty-one official PGA Tour events in 1945.

His stroke average that year was 68.33, including nineteen consecutive rounds in the 60s. His official prize money, in cash and in war bonds if held to maturity, was $63,335, a bonanza in that era. Never before or since has a golfer been so dominant in a calendar year.

But 1945 was merely Nelson's best year, not his only year.

As a young touring pro out of Fort Worth, Texas, he won the 1937 Masters; the 1939 U.S. Open in a playoff with Craig Wood and Denny Shute; the 1940 PGA Championship; and the 1942 Masters in a playoff with Ben Hogan; as well as the 1945 PGA during his streak. His career total of fifty-one PGA Tour victories ranks fifth, behind Sam Snead's eighty-one, Jack Nicklaus's seventy, Ben Hogan's sixty-three, and Arnold Palmer's sixty. But those four golfers were out there for anywhere from twenty to thirty years. He was out there for only a dozen.

After the 1946 season, he decided to stop playing competitive golf and buy what he would call his Fairway Ranch in Roanoke, Texas, not far from what is now the Dallas-Fort Worth Airport.

"I've never looked back," he often said of leaving golf at the relatively young age of thirty-four. "Nobody understands it, but I never did feel I quit too soon. I accomplished everything I set out to do. People say it's too bad that I won all those tournaments and the prize money was so small. I'm not envious. It was fun playing when I played. I had been under a lot of pressure and I knew I was going to be a rancher."

Never before or since has a golfer been known to hit the ball so straight so often. And in life, he's been even straighter. He's never been heard to use bad language. He's had maybe a dozen drinks. He's never smoked.

"If whenever people mention great players, they think of me, that would be nice," Nelson once said, "but I prefer being remembered as a nice man with a lot of integrity, as somebody people could love and trust, as being friendly and a good Christian man. If I had made twenty million dollars when I played golf, I probably wouldn't be as good of a man as I am now. If I made all the money in the world, my life wouldn't have been improved on."

Nelson, who was television's first golf analyst, is also remembered for winning the 1939 U.S. Open that Sam Snead didn't win.

"I've never resented that," Nelson said, "and I'll tell you why. I think the record would prove that most Opens are lost rather than won. It's just that Sam never won the Open and that's why they remember him losing the Open that I won."

But with a swing as smooth as maple syrup, Samuel Jackson Snead won just about everything but the Open.

As a barefoot farm boy near Hot Springs, Virginia, he cut swamp maple branches into golf clubs and sank tomato cans into the ground for cups. When he graduated to real clubs, he soon emerged as a local legend while working as an assistant pro at the Cascades course for twenty dollars a month. After winning both the West Virginia Open and the West Virginia PGA in 1936, he decided to join the PGA Tour in 1936, winning his second event, the Oakland Open, and then the original Bing Crosby National Pro-Am. When he was shown a copy of the *New York Times* with his picture in it, he shook his head.

"How'd they get that?" he asked. "I've never been in New York."

He soon learned that photos could be transmitted to anywhere in the world, but he never had to learn how to swing a golf club. He was golf's Natural.

"I just made my swing," he often said, "as simple as I could."

He would win a record eighty-one PGA Tour events, including seven majors—the 1946, 1949, and 1954 Masters; the 1946 British

Open; and the 1942, 1949, and 1951 PGA Championships. When he won the 1965 Greater Greensboro Open at age fifty-two, he became the oldest to win an official PGA Tour event. It also was his eighth Greater Greensboro victory, the record for one tournament.

"Where Sam excels," Jack Nicklaus has said, "is in being able to enjoy the game. He could play virtually every day without going stale, which is not true of most players."

Snead would win another fifty to seventy unofficial tournaments as well as fourteen Senior events, including the 1980 Commemorative Pro-Am at the Newport (Rhode Island) Country Club. Then sixty-eight years old, he shot 68-67 to defeat a field of touring pros who were mostly in their fifties.

"I shot my age," he liked to say, "every year since I was sixty."

While wearing his usual coconut-straw hat, he shot his best official score, 59, at age forty-seven in the 1959 Greenbrier Open. At age seventy-one and bothered by depth-perception problems in his eyes, he shot 60 at the Lower Cascades course in his Hot Springs, Virginia, hometown. And when the PGA Tour issued its all-time rankings in 1989, he was first, Nicklaus second.

"We got to go by the record," Snead said. "Put the record down and let the chips fall. Nicklaus is where he should be. Second. I like that."

But for all his success, Snead also will be remembered as the best golfer never to win the U.S. Open, a tournament he nearly won twice.

In the 1939 U.S. Open that Nelson eventually won, Snead needed only to par the last 2 holes to win. But at tournaments in those years, there were no scoreboards showing the hole-by-hole progress of the leaders. After he bogied the 17th hole, his drive on the par-5 final hole hooked into the rough; then he topped a 2-wood into a fairway bunker, scuffed his next two shots into bunkers, and finally blasted onto the green only to 3-putt for a disastrous 8 for 74 and fifth place.

"If I'd had a leaderboard," Snead has said, "I'd have played that hole differently."

In the 1947 U.S. Open at the St. Louis Country Club, he holed a 20-foot birdie putt to tie Lew Worsham but lost their 18-hole play-off after Worsham called for a measurement of their putts on the 18th hole to determine who was away. Snead's downhill putt was 30.5 inches from the cup, Worsham's uphill putt 29.5 inches. Snead missed. Worsham made.

"The measurement broke my concentration," Snead said, "but I never blamed Lew. We were great friends."

That missed putt would turn out to be Snead's last real opportunity to win the U.S. Open, primarily because Ben Hogan dominated most of the next decade. From 1948 to 1953, Hogan, who had grown up in the same caddie yard in Fort Worth with Byron Nelson, won eight of his nine major titles: four U.S. Opens, two Masters, one British Open, and one PGA to add to his 1946 PGA title. He would be honored by a ticker-tape parade up Broadway in New York City in 1953 after sweeping three major titles that year—the Masters, the U.S. Open, and the British Open.

Ben Hogan rides high at his ticker-tape parade in New York City.

"But my greatest accomplishment," he said, "was being able to make a living playing golf after going broke twice."

Hogan had a shaky start on the PGA Tour before emerging as its leading money winner in 1940, 1941, 1942, and 1946, but in 1948 he won the U.S. Open at Riviera in Los Angeles and his second PGA title. On February 2, 1949, as he was driving along a foggy highway near Van Horn, Texas, with his wife, Valerie, a Greyhound bus pulled out from behind a trailer truck and smashed head-on into his car. To protect his wife, Hogan threw himself across her lap. She suffered bruised ribs, bruised legs, and a black eye, but his injuries were far worse: a double fracture of the pelvis, a fractured collarbone, a fractured left ankle, and a chipped rib.

He would live, but would he ever regain his strength and skill as a golfer?

Sturdy but small at 5–8 and 138 pounds, his body had been battered, his feel for a golf club shattered. But his determination was stronger than ever—not just to play tournament golf again, but to play it better than he ever had. He returned to the PGA Tour early in 1950, trudging on weary legs. In June, at Merion outside Philadelphia, he won that year's U.S. Open in an 18-hole playoff, shooting a 1-under-par 69 to Lloyd Mangrum's 73 and George Fazio's 75.

"Of all my victories," he said later, "Merion meant the most because it proved I could still win."

In his flat white linen cap, Hogan kept winning. In 1951, he won the Masters and then the U.S. Open with a 3-under-par 67 in the final round at Oakland Hills outside Detroit, a treacherous course with tangled rough that had the other golfers groaning.

"I'm glad," he said at the trophy presentation, "that I brought this course, this monster, to its knees."

After a relatively empty year in 1952, Hogan entered only six tournaments in 1953 and won five, including his Triple Crown in the Masters, the U.S. Open at Oakmont outside Pittsburgh, and the

Ben Hogan
surveys a putt
at the Masters.

British Open at Carnoustie, Scotland, where he was known as the Wee Icemon. Carnoustie isn't far from St. Andrews, but he didn't bother traveling less than two hours to play the Old Course.

"I didn't have time to go to St. Andrews," he explained. "I was there for one purpose."

His purpose in Scotland had been to win the British Open, period, end of trip. Ben Hogan was always a man of purpose, a man who believed in practice and more practice rather than the mysterious "secret" that he supposedly had in swinging a golf club.

"The secret's in the dirt," he once said, meaning the dirt of the practice range. "Dig it out of the dirt."

He and his wife, Valerie, had their friends in their golf travels, but on the golf course he seldom spoke, seldom strayed from peering down the fairway to check where the wind was blowing, seldom strayed from his concentration on the next shot or the next putt.

"About all Ben ever said in a tournament," Sam Snead has often said, "was, 'Good luck' on the first tee and 'You're away' a few times after that."

During the 1947 Masters, Hogan and one of his best friends, Claude Harmon, were playing together. On the 12th hole, Harmon got a hole in one. But they walked off the green together in silence. No mention of the hole in one. No congratulations.

"I don't remember Ben saying anything," Harmon said later. "My ace didn't help him, and he wasn't going to come out of his shell."

Hogan's concentration applied to his clubs, even to his golf balls. After a practice round before the 1955 U.S. Open at Olympic in San Francisco, he was seen peering through a magnifying glass at, one by one, a shipment of several dozen new golf balls. He put most of the balls back in their boxes, but every so often he tossed a ball aside.

"Some of these balls," he explained, "have a little too much paint in the dimples."

Several days later, Hogan thought he had won at Olympic for what would have been his record fifth U.S. Open, but with birdies at the 15th and 18th holes, Jack Fleck, a virtually unknown pro at two municipal courses in Davenport, Iowa, forced an 18-hole playoff the next day. Hardly anybody in golf had heard of Fleck, but Hogan had.

"He must be good," Hogan said. "He uses Hogan clubs."

Several weeks earlier, Fleck had traveled to Fort Worth to obtain a set of Hogan clubs. Hogan had let him into the factory. And in their playoff, Fleck shot 69, Hogan 72.

"I can't believe it, Ben," Fleck said as they walked off the 18th green. "I can't believe it."

Not many other golf people believed it either, but an unknown, never really to be heard from again, had defeated Ben Hogan in a U.S. Open playoff. Hogan would play in a few more U.S. Opens, but he would contend in only one. In 1960 at Cherry Hills outside Denver, he had a chance to win until his wedge in the final round spun back into the narrow moat surrounding the 17th green. At the 1967 Masters, at age fifty-four, his third-round 66 with a 30 on the back 9 would be his last hurrah.

"I always outworked everybody," he once said. "Work never bothered me like it bothers some people."

In time, Jack Nicklaus would be hailed as history's best golfer, but when Tommy Bolt, the 1958 U.S. Open champion, was asked to compare Hogan to Nicklaus, he answered for all the golfers of the Hogan era.

"All I know is," Bolt said in his Texas twang, "I've seen Nicklaus watch Hogan practice. I've never seen Hogan watch Nicklaus practice."

ARNOLD PALMER HAD SHOT A 2-OVER-PAR 72 IN Saturday morning's third round of the 1960 U.S. Open and now, as he munched on a cheeseburger in the Cherry Hills locker room in Denver, he was in 15th place, 7 strokes behind leader Mike Souchak, 5 behind Julius Boros, Dow Finsterwald, and Jerry Barber, and 4 behind Ben Hogan and a twenty-year-old amateur, Jack Nicklaus. But as Palmer awaited the final round in what was then known as Open Saturday, a 36-hole finish, he was thinking about how he could win.

"I'll drive the first green and get a birdie or an eagle," he said. "I might shoot 65. What'll that do?"

"Nothing," said Bob Drum, the golf writer from the *Pittsburgh Press* who chronicled the life and times of the then thirty-year-old touring pro from nearby Latrobe, Pennsylvania. "You're too far back."

"But a 65 would give me 280," Palmer said. "Doesn't 280 always win the Open?"

"Yeah, when Hogan shoots it," Drum snorted. "Go shoot 73. I'll see you later."

Leaving some of his cheeseburger, Palmer stormed out of the locker room toward the tee of the 346-yard 1st hole, a downhill par-4 guarded by a patch of rough in front of the green. All week, other golfers had not dared to challenge that rough, but now Palmer did. His tee shot somehow bounced through the rough onto the green and stopped about 20 feet away from the pin.

His eagle putt slid by the hole, but he tapped in for his birdie.

On the 2nd hole, he chipped in from 35 feet for another birdie.

On the 3rd, he spun a wedge to within 1 foot. Another birdie.

On the 4th, he holed an 18-foot putt to go 4 under after only 4 holes, and his gallery, known as Arnie's Army, was on the march. So was Bob Drum, hurrying out onto the course.

By the 8th hole, Palmer was 5 under par for the round and even par for the tournament.

After the final putt of his 30–35 for the 65 and 280 he had demanded of himself, Palmer whirled his white visor into the Rocky Mountain air. He would win by 2 strokes over Nicklaus, whose 39 on the back 9 gave him a 71, as the other contenders dropped away. Souchak soared to 75, Barber to 74. Hogan, Boros, and Finsterwald each had a shaky 73.

In a span of seven seasons from 1958 to 1964, Arnold Palmer would win all seven of his major titles, including four Masters and two British Opens, but with that 65 in the 1960 U.S. Open, he had put the word *charge* into golf's vocabulary.

"When I started on the Tour, I saw guys who were great from tee to green but who never won," he once said, referring to

Arnold Palmer whips off his visor after his final-round 65 that won the 1960 U.S. Open at Cherry Hills.

Arnold Palmer danced to four Masters triumphs.

his rookie year in 1955 after having won the 1954 United States Amateur. "I didn't want to be one of those players. What I wanted to be was one of the great players who hit it into the woods over here, then hit it into the ditch over there, then hit it into the hole on the next shot."

Growing up as the son of Milfred ("Deacon") Palmer, the club pro at the Latrobe Country Club, he couldn't play with the members or even during the day when the members were around. He had to play whenever the course was empty, usually in the morning or at dusk. But every so often, when the women members were playing, he would sit with his driver near the tee of a certain hole with a ditch about 100 yards away. That ditch intimidated some of the women members.

"Good morning, ladies," he would say. "I'll hit your ball over the ditch for a nickel."

He earned a pocketful of nickels that way, and soon he was breaking par at Latrobe.

"My father told me," he once said, "to always figure that the other guy is going to make the best shot in the world or make the putt, and to just figure that you're going to make it better and more often."

More often than not, Arnold Palmer did just that. In so doing, he popularized golf as never before—one reason why he was crowned golf's King by his contemporaries.

Over more than four decades, he won sixty PGA Tour events, thirteen other tournaments around the world, and ten Senior PGA Tour events while emerging as a multimillionaire conglomerate. Marketed by his longtime friend and attorney, Mark McCormack, who constructed the worldwide International Management Group around him, he has accomplished even more off the course. Arnold Palmer Enterprises designs golf courses, manages instruction schools, and controls aviation and automobile dealerships. He was the first touring pro to own and fly his own plane. But more than anything else, he played golf like a heavyweight boxing champion or a linebacker.

"If I ever had an eight-foot putt and everything I owned depended on it," Bobby Jones once said, "I'd want Arnold Palmer to take it for me."

But part of Palmer's charm was that he might miss that 8-foot putt. For all his dramatic triumphs, he lost just as theatrically. At the 1961 Masters, he was on the 18th tee in the final round with a 1-stroke lead over Gary Player when a spectator congratulated him on being the first golfer to earn the green jacket at Augusta National in two consecutive years.

"Thank you," Palmer said, smiling.

Minutes later, after a good drive into the fairway, he skidded his 7-iron approach into a bunker, blasted out over the green, chipped 15 feet past the cup, and 2-putted for a double-bogey 6 that put the green jacket on Player.

"Accepting those congratulations near the tee was my mistake," he said. "I broke my concentration."

He might have won three other U.S. Open titles, but he lost in an 18-hole playoff each time. The most haunting of those three defeats developed in 1966 at Olympic in San Francisco after he was 7 strokes ahead of Billy Casper with 9 holes to play, and then 6 strokes ahead with 6 holes to play. He finished with a 71 as Casper's 68 created a tie at 278. In the playoff, Casper shot 69, Palmer 73.

In a 1963 three-way playoff at The Country Club outside Boston, he shot 76 and Jacky Cupit 73 as Julius Boros won with 70.

But the defining loss in Palmer's career occurred in the 1962 U.S. Open at Oakmont outside Pittsburgh, not far from his Latrobe home. Needing 4 to get down from the edge of the 9th green in the final round, his 71 enabled Jack Nicklaus to force a playoff, which the twenty-two-year-old rookie pro won, 71 to 74.

"He's a big, strong dude," Palmer said of his conqueror.

That big, strong dude's domination had begun, but because of Palmer's popularity, some people at first openly resented Nicklaus's success and hooted at his hefty weight.

He was called Fat Jack and Ohio Fats. But eventually, those names evolved into Big Jack and the Golden Bear.

Jack Nicklaus would join Ben Hogan, Bobby Jones, and Willie Anderson as the only golfers to win four U.S. Open titles. Including his two U.S. Amateur titles in 1959 and 1961, he won a total of twenty major championships: his record-sharing four U.S. Opens, a record six Masters, three British Opens, and five PGA Championships. He won seventy times on the PGA Tour (second to Sam Snead's record eighty-one), fourteen times around the world, and ten times on the Senior PGA Tour, including the U.S. Senior Open twice. He was the PGA Tour's leading money winner eight times.

To appreciate his twenty major titles, consider that Bobby Jones is next with thirteen, followed by Walter Hagen with eleven, Ben Hogan and Gary Player with nine, and Tom Watson with eight.

Consider, too, that Nicklaus won each of the four major championships at least three times while none of the other three to sweep those Grand Slam events (Sarazen, Hogan, and Player) won every major even twice.

Jack Nicklaus

No wonder Jack Nicklaus, who won major titles from ages nineteen to forty-six over a span of more than a quarter of a century, is deservedly considered by most historians to be the best golfer ever.

Sturdy at 5–11 and 190 pounds, he arrived on the PGA Tour in 1962 as its strongest and longest hitter. He also arrived as the first touring pro to play by yardage that he or his caddie had measured. He had learned that at the 1961 U.S. Amateur from Deane Beman, later the PGA Tour commissioner, who had learned it from Gene Andrews, a California amateur. After winning the 1962 U.S. Open at Oakmont as a rookie pro, Nicklaus displayed a scorecard with his yardage notes.

"It takes the guesswork out of the game," he said. "In practice rounds, I write down the location of the traps and ridges and trees and the distances from them to the front and back of the greens. Then when I see where the pin is, I know exactly how far I am from the pin and what club I should use."

Other touring pros soon were playing by yardage. But none of them could play as consistently well as this blond son of a Columbus, Ohio, pharmacist, a member of the Scioto Country Club there. That's where Bobby Jones won the 1926 U.S. Open, prompting Nicklaus's ambition to emulate his golf role model.

"I was always competitive," he once said, "but my father kept me at it, like the way he taught me how to run. I was in the sixth grade and I wasn't very fast. I was sort of a chunky kid. He said, 'If you're going to play football and basketball, you've got to be fast. You've got to learn how to run on your toes. If you want to learn how, go out for track.' So I went out for track in the seventh grade and I learned how to run. I ran the hundred and the two-twenty and the relays and did the high jump. By the time I finished track, I was the fastest guy in the seventh and eighth grades. That's the sort of thing my father did for me."

His competitive attitude was never more apparent than in the final event of the 1964 PGA Tour, the Cajun Classic in Lafayette, Louisiana, a tournament he normally would have skipped.

With that year's leading money-winner title at stake, both Nicklaus and Palmer entered. Nicklaus was trailing Palmer by $318.82, but his second-place finish in that tournament brought his total for the year to $113,284.50, which edged Palmer's total of $113,203.37.

"It's a difference of only $81.13," Nicklaus said, "but the idea of being first was worth a lot more than that."

Even with the money title, Nicklaus had considered 1964 a bad year, his first as a pro in which he did not win a major. He had finished second in the Masters, the British Open, and the PGA, but for him second might as well have been twenty-second. But in the 1965 Masters, he stormed to a 9-stroke victory over both Palmer and Player with a record 271 score, 17 under par.

"He plays a game," Bobby Jones said at the Masters green-jacket ceremony, "with which I am not familiar."

Nobody else was familiar with that game either. But two months later, Gary Player, a little South African who usually wore black shirts and black slacks that made him feel stronger, justified his niche next to Nicklaus and Palmer in what was known as golf's Big Three and also supplied further proof that golfers from outside the United States were capable of winning several major championships.

"Even as a youngster, the British Open was always the most important tournament to me," Player often said. "The links are where golf started, and the elements make it the most difficult tournament to win."

Growing up near Johannesburg, he was fifteen when his father, a 2-handicap left-handed golfer, gave him a set of clubs. He hurried to the nearby Virginia Park course and parred the first 3 holes he ever played, an omen for a golfer who would describe himself as a "citizen of the world" and would grow to only 5–7 and 150 pounds. He relied on exercise and a diet featuring fruit and nuts to maintain his strength. As a golfer, he relied on accuracy.

"Golfers from countries around the world learn to hit the ball straighter than Americans do," he said. "In our countries, we have rough that you would just not believe, and you have absolutely no chance unless you can hit the ball straight. So we learn to hit it straight first. Then we learn to hit it a little harder."

Player hit the ball so straight, he won his first of three British Opens in 1959, his first of three Masters in 1961, and his first of two PGA Championships in 1962. When he won the 1965 U.S. Open at Bellerive near St. Louis in an 18-hole playoff with Kel Nagle of Australia, he joined Sarazen and Hogan as the winner of all four modern major championships; Nicklaus would join them later.

"The great highlight of my life," Player once said, "was completing that career Grand Slam."

At that U.S. Open, he fulfilled a promise he had made to a USGA official years before.

"I promised the USGA," he said, "that when I won the Open, I would give the money back. I'm a foreigner here. The American people have treated me so well, I want to give something back to them."

He did just that. Of his twenty-five-thousand-dollar first prize, he gave twenty thousand dollars to junior golf, five thousand to cancer research.

Player, always fit and always positive, would go on to win the Masters in 1974 and again in 1978 at the age of forty-two, which at the time was considered old for a competitive golfer. That is, until Jack Nicklaus won the 1986 Masters at the age of forty-six. Having not won a major since 1980, when he won both the U.S. Open and the PGA, the Golden Bear appeared to be well past his peak. But he didn't think so. The day before the 1986 Masters, he was asked to rate the three most difficult shots on the back 9 on Sunday with the tournament at stake, but declined.

"I don't want to be standing over a shot on Sunday," he explained, "and say to myself that I told you this is the most difficult shot on the back nine."

Never having a negative thought was as much a part of Nicklaus's thinking as his competitive attitude. And on that back 9 on Sunday, he shot 30 with an eagle 3 at the 15th hole, a birdie 2 at the 16th (after just missing a hole in one), and a birdie 3 at the 17th. At forty-six, he won his sixth Masters with his oldest son, Jackie, as his caddie.

"Considering my age," he said, "the state of my game, and the fact that I had Jackie by my side, it's hard, at least for me, to think of a better moment."

But as dramatic as that moment was, to all those who had followed Jack Nicklaus's career, it was merely one of so many wonderful moments.

His putter high, Jack Nicklaus watches his birdie putt disappear on the 17th green during the final round of the 1986 Masters.

NEAR THE 1ST TEE OF THE 1971 U.S. OPEN PLAYOFF with Jack Nicklaus at Merion outside Philadelphia, Lee Trevino reached into his golf bag for a new golf glove but pulled out a three-foot toy rubber snake.

"I'd bought it at a zoo for my daughter. I don't know how it got in my bag," Trevino later explained. "But when I held it up, everybody laughed, including Jack, and he asked me to throw it to him, so I did."

Nicklaus jumped, as if he were afraid of the snake, prompting some people to assume that Trevino had unnerved him. If that were the case, Nicklaus disproved it with a par on the 1st hole to Trevino's bogey for a quick 1-stroke lead. But on the 2nd hole, Nicklaus didn't recover from a bunker and took a bogey 6. On the 3rd, he flubbed another sand shot and took a double-bogey 5. Trevino, who called himself the Merry Mex because of his Mexican heritage, would win the playoff, 68 to 71, for his second U.S. Open championship. Not that he was surprised.

"I believe," he had said in the locker room before the playoff, "the Mex will get Big Jack today."

For all of Lee Trevino's six major titles (consecutive British Opens in 1971 and 1972 and two PGA Championships in 1974 and 1984 in addition to his two U.S. Opens), he has always insisted that Jack Nicklaus is "the greatest golfer who ever lived; you got to be lucky to beat him." More often than not, Trevino, chunky at 5–8 and 180 pounds, was as good as he was lucky. And yet he has always thanked Nicklaus for inspiring him early in 1971.

"Jack told me, 'I hope you never find out how well you can play. If you do, it will be trouble for all of us,'" Trevino often said. "That word of encouragement changed my life. It stopped me from being the nervous character I was. I realized I could reach the peak."

As a youngster growing up in Dallas with his mother and his grandfather, a Mexican immigrant gravedigger, in a house without electricity and plumbing, Lee Buck Trevino faced a long, hard climb to the peak. He quit school in the eighth grade, worked on the maintenance crew of a local course while learning to play golf, joined the Marines at seventeen, polished his game in Okinawa, then returned to Dallas to work at the Tenison Park course during the day. At night, he worked at a pitch-and-putt course, where he wagered on himself swinging a quart-sized Dr Pepper bottle wrapped in adhesive tape instead of a normal golf club.

"I never lost a bet using that bottle," he often said with a laugh.

In real golf bets in the Dallas-Fort Worth area, he seldom lost either. His reputation as a hustler attracted a job offer at the Horizon Hills Country Club in El Paso, Texas, as an assistant pro at thirty dollars a week, and the opportunity to play what he liked to call "sociable" golf, meaning money matches, notably one with Raymond Floyd, then a young touring pro who would win the PGA twice as well as the Masters and the U.S. Open. Those money matches honed Trevino's style for duels with Nicklaus, Gary Player, and others in major tournaments.

"I like head-to-head," he would say, "because I was a hustler all my life."

That life changed at the 1967 U.S. Open at Baltusrol in Springfield, New Jersey, when Trevino, a virtual unknown, finished fifth. The next year at Oak Hill in Rochester, New York, he was the first to shoot in the 60s in all four rounds of the U.S. Open (67-68-69-69), winning by 4 strokes while wearing a red shirt, black slacks, red socks, and black shoes in the final round. In 1971, he completed a rare double, adding the British Open at Royal Birkdale to his U.S. Open title at

Lee Trevino arrived at the 1968 U.S. Open.

Merion. The next year, he repeated in the British Open at Muirfield, ending Nicklaus's bid that year for a modern Grand Slam.

"Jack," he said, "is the toughest player there is to beat, the best in the world."

Trevino, however, had beaten Nicklaus again, as he would in the final round of the 1974 PGA at Tanglewood in Clemmons, North

Carolina. But during a rain-and-lightning delay at the 1975 Western Open in Chicago, he was leaning against his golf bag while sitting on the grass alongside a lake near Butler National's 13th green. Suddenly a lightning bolt struck the lake and traveled along the ground, through the steel shafts of his clubs, and into his body.

"I should have been dead," he said, "but I wasn't."

The lightning aggravated his back ailments, prompting spinal-disc surgery in 1976. But in 1980, he collected a record fifth Vardon Trophy with a scoring average of 69.73, the best since Sam Snead's 69.23 in 1950. And in 1984 at Shoal Creek outside Birmingham, Alabama, he won another PGA Championship.

"It's nice," he said, "that an old guy can still beat those young guys."

One of those young guys was Tom Watson, who had already won eight majors, including five British Opens, notably at Turnberry in 1977 in a duel with Nicklaus that many historians consider golf's most memorable medal-play match. Through the first three rounds, each had shot the same score, 68-70-65, but by the 209-yard 15th hole in the final round, Nicklaus was 1 stroke ahead, with a realistic chance to go 2 ahead.

Watson's 4-iron had missed the green, stopping on a hardpan up-slope about 60 feet from the flagstick. Nicklaus's 4-iron had spun to 12 feet below the cup.

Using a putter, Watson rapped his ball but appeared to have rapped it too hard. Thinking the ball would slide well past the cup, Nicklaus leaned over to place his ball at his marker when he heard a thunk. Watson's ball had hit the flagstick and disappeared into the cup. Birdie 2. When the Golden Bear missed his 12-footer and tapped in for par, they were tied at 11 under for the tournament with 3 holes remaining. Now, on the 16th tee, the twenty-seven-year-old Watson turned to the thirty-seven-year-old Golden Bear.

"This is what it's all about, isn't it?" Watson said.

Nicklaus smiled. More than anyone, he knew that this indeed is what golf is all about: two great golfers at their best in one of the world's best tournaments. After each parred the 16th, they went to the 17th, a par 5 of 515 yards. After each hit a big drive, Watson drilled a 3-iron onto the green, only 12 feet away. Nicklaus pushed a 4-iron into brownish rough, about 50 feet up a slope, then chipped to within 4 feet.

Watson made his 12-footer for a birdie 4; Nicklaus missed his 4-footer to drop 1 stroke behind.

On the 18th, a par 4 of 434 yards, Nicklaus holed a 30-foot birdie putt, forcing Watson to study his 3-footer for a birdie. If he missed, they would be tied, requiring an 18-hole playoff the next day. But he made it for a 65, to Nicklaus's 66.

"I gave you my best shot," Nicklaus told Watson, "but it wasn't good enough. You were better."

Watson had been better at the Masters that year too. His 20-foot birdie putt at the 17th as Nicklaus bogied the 18th had created his 2-stroke victory. He conquered the pressure and won, much the same way he had overcome the pressure as a seven-year-old when he was told he couldn't play at a municipal course while on a Colorado vacation.

"The kid can't play," the man behind the counter said. "He's too young."

His father, Ray Watson, a top golfer at their hometown Kansas City Country Club, explained that little Tom had taken lessons and knew how to play, but the man behind the counter wouldn't budge.

"Sorry," he said. "The kid's too young."

"I'll make a deal with you," Ray Watson said. "I noticed that on the first hole, there's a ditch about forty yards out. If my son hits his tee shot over that ditch, will you let him play?"

"Fair enough," the man said.

Taking his 3-wood, little Tom whacked his tee shot far over the ditch, about 100 yards down the fairway.

"The kid can play," the man said.

At thirteen, that kid shot a 67. At fourteen, he was the Kansas City match-play champion. At fifteen, on the 1st tee in an exhibition with Arnold Palmer, he crushed a 270-yard drive.

"Who is this kid?" Palmer asked.

At twenty-five, that kid would win his first major, the 1975 British Open, in an 18-hole play-off with Australia's Jack Newton after holing a 25-foot birdie putt on Carnoustie's 18th green to tie. In addition to his 1977 title, he also won the British Open in 1980, 1982, and 1983. And at the 1982 U.S. Open at Pebble Beach on California's Monterey Peninsula, he stabbed Nicklaus again. With a 69 for 284, Nicklaus, already in the scorer's tent behind the 18th green, knew that Watson needed a par-par finish to tie him. And when Watson pulled his 1-iron into the tangled rough to the left of the green on the 209-yard 17th hole, Nicklaus knew he would win a record fifth U.S. Open if Watson were to bogey the 17th and par the 18th.

But now, back on the 17th, when Watson's caddie, Bruce

Tom Watson

Tom Watson celebrates holing out from the rough at Pebble Beach in the 1982 U.S. Open with his caddie, Bruce Edwards.

Edwards, said, "Get it close," Watson replied, "I'm not going to get it close. I'm going to make it."

Watson did just that, lofting the ball with his sand-wedge out of the rough, then watching it roll across the green and disappear into the cup. Birdie 2. To win, all he needed now was a par at the 18th along the rocky rim of Carmel Bay. Playing safely with a 3-wood off the tee, then a 7-iron and a 9-iron, he lagged a 25-foot putt that dropped for another birdie. Watson had won by 2 strokes, and his holed sand-wedge out of the rough at the 17th would be remembered as one of golf's most memorable shots.

"It was," Watson said, "the best shot of my life, a shot that had more meaning to me than any other shot of my career."

Some people thought it had been a lucky shot, but Watson disagreed, citing an old saying: The harder you work, the luckier you get.

"I practiced that shot," he said. "At the Open, where they let the grass grow high around the greens, you need that shot."

As Tom Watson discovered to his dismay, few have had more shots than Seve Ballesteros, the dashing Spaniard who revitalized European golf. As a youngster, the three-time British Open champion and two-time Masters winner had learned to play by hitting balls with one club, a 3-iron, around the Real Pedreña course and off the wet sand of the beach near his home not far from the fishing port of Santander on Spain's northern coast.

"The Real Pedreña clubhouse was only about three hundred yards from our house, the second hole about one hundred twenty yards away," his brother Manuel said. "Seve would go there with his three-iron—I think it was one of mine. When he was twelve, he won the caddie championship. When he was fifteen, he shot his first 65."

When Severiano Ballesteros was nineteen, he shared second place with Jack Nicklaus in the 1976 British Open at Royal Lytham and St. Annes, alerting the golf world that he would be somebody special. At twenty-two, in the 1979 British Open, he emerged as the youngest player in this century to win the coveted claret-jug silver trophy while missing the fairway with his tee shot on all but 2 holes. On the 16th hole, after pushing his tee shot into what the British call a car park and finding his ball under a white sports car, he received a free drop, then floated a sand-wedge to within 20 feet of the cup.

"If all the time it is fairway, fairway, fairway," he once said, "it must be very boring."

Seve Ballesteros was never boring. Some people mistook his

Seve Ballesteros winning the 1979 British Open

ability as an escape artist for luck when it was really genius. At a trick-shot exhibition, Peter Jacobsen, one of the PGA Tour's top players, watched Ballesteros stand only on his left foot and hit a 300-yard drive, then stand only on his right foot and hit a 300-yard drive.

"And both of them," Jacobsen said, "went dead straight."

Ballesteros was never straighter than in the 1983 Masters' final round. Hitting arrows off the tee, he holed an 18-foot birdie putt at the 1st hole and a 15-foot eagle putt at the 2nd. After a 2-putt par at the 3rd, he drilled a 2-iron to within 2 feet on the 4th for another birdie. Over 4 holes, he had needed only 12 strokes to go 4 under par in what would be a 69. Watson later compared his reaction to that of a boxer being knocked out in the first round.

"Those first four holes were the best I ever played in my life," Ballesteros said after earning his second green jacket. "If people say I'm lucky after that, I want to be a lucky golfer for many years."

The next year, in the 1984 British Open at St. Andrews, the handsome Spaniard victimized Watson again. Tied for the lead, Ballesteros was playing ahead of Watson as they came to the 17th, the famous Road Hole with a tee shot threatened on the right by an old railroad shed and the Old Course hotel grounds, then a second to a green with a pot bunker on the left and an old rock wall beyond the road behind the green.

Ballesteros drove into the left rough, then floated a 6-iron to within 30 feet for a 2-putt par. Watson drove into the fairway, but his 2-iron bounced over the green and settled about 2 feet from the wall. His chip skidded 30 feet beyond the cup. Two putts, bogey. Up ahead, Ballesteros birdied the 18th, floating a wedge over the Valley of Sin and sinking a 15-foot birdie putt. He won by 2 strokes.

"If Seve plays well and the rest of us play well," said two-time Masters winner Ben Crenshaw, "Seve wins."

Ballesteros would add another British Open in a return to Royal Lytham and St. Annes in 1988, a year that showed how far Europe had rebounded in golf. Scotland's Sandy Lyle won the Masters, and

England's Nick Faldo forced an 18-hole playoff with Curtis Strange in the U.S. Open at The Country Club.

But more than anyone else, Ballesteros had inspired Europe's golfers in the Ryder Cup matches between the PGA Tour's best players and the European Tour's best.

From the time the Ryder Cup matches originated in 1927, United States pros, from Walter Hagen and Gene Sarazen to Ben Hogan and Sam Snead to Arnold Palmer and Jack Nicklaus, had dominated the biannual matches. But in 1985, the European team, led by Spain's Ballesteros and Manuel Piñero, stunned the United States team, 16 1/2 to 11 1/2 in the 28 matches.

It wasn't a fluke. The Europeans would win in 1987, 1989, 1995, and, dramatically, in 1997 when the matches were held in Spain for the first time, and Europe's captain, driving a cart everywhere at Valderrama to exhort his players, was Severiano Ballesteros.

"Every time you were thinking, What can I do here?" said Spain's Ignacio Garrido, "Seve would appear out of nowhere and tell you what to do."

It had taken a century for Scotland's gift to be unwrapped in America, but overall the best golfers in Europe now were considered to be as skilled as the best golfers in the United States.

Seve Ballesteros, the captain of the winning European Ryder Cup team in 1997 at Valderrama, surveys the scene he created.

TIGER WOODS ARRIVED AT AUGUSTA NATIONAL FOR THE 1997 Masters as a twenty-one-year-old rookie pro with the same determination he had displayed there as a nineteen-year-old U.S. Amateur champion two years earlier.

"I'm here," he said quietly but firmly, "to win the tournament."

Woods didn't win the Masters as an amateur, but in 1997 he won it not only as a rookie pro but also as no other golfer ever had. With a Masters record 18-under-par total of 270, he won by 12 strokes, the largest margin of victory in a major tournament in modern times. He reminded golf historians of Bobby Jones's memorable description of Jack Nicklaus's record 271 in winning the 1965 Masters.

"He plays a game," the Masters patron saint said of Nicklaus, "with which I am not familiar."

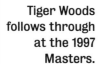

Tiger Woods follows through at the 1997 Masters.

After Woods's performance, Nicklaus was asked to assess the young man who had broken the Masters record he had shared with Raymond Floyd, who also shot 271 in his 1976 victory.

"Let's face it," the fifty-seven-year-old Golden Bear said graciously of Woods. "It's his time now."

The year before, Nicklaus, the six-time Masters winner, had predicted Tiger's time after having played a practice round at the Masters with the then twenty-year-old U.S. Amateur champion and Arnold Palmer, the four-time Masters winner.

"Arnold and I both agreed," Nicklaus said, "that you could take his Masters and my Masters and add them together, and this kid should win more than that."

In the 1997 Masters, this kid showed he has the talent and the competitive makeup needed to win major tournaments. As the only child of an African-American lieutenant colonel in the U.S. Army during the Vietnam war and a Thai mother, he has also lifted golf to a new sociological level.

Charlie Sifford, the first African-American to hold a PGA Tour card

"I'm the first," he said, meaning the first golfer of color to put on the Masters green jacket, "but I'm not the pioneer. Charlie Sifford, Lee Elder, Teddy Rhodes—those guys paved the way for me to be here. I thank them. If it wasn't for them, I might not have had the chance to play here."

After watching Woods win the 1997 Masters on television in his Kingwood, Texas, home, Sifford reacted as if he himself had earned a green jacket.

"It's a wonderful thing for golf, never mind the racial thing,"

Sifford said. "This kid is doing what I wanted to do, but never had the chance."

As one of the few black pros in previous years, Sifford, like Elder and Rhodes, had suffered racial discrimination. Sifford won the 1967 Greater Hartford Open and the 1969 Los Angeles Open, but in those years before a PGA Tour victory earned an automatic Masters invitation, he was ignored. Elder emerged as the first black to play in the Masters, in 1975, after having won the 1974 Pensacola Open, but Rhodes was barred from PGA-sponsored tournaments in the fifties and sixties because of a Caucasian-only clause that wasn't erased until 1961.

Lee Elder

Other black pros had struggled too—Jim Dent, Calvin Peete, Jim Thorpe, and Pete Brown, to name four.

But none had arrived on the PGA Tour with the credentials that Woods had as a three-time U.S. Amateur champion and a three-time U.S. Junior Amateur champion, a 1996 NCAA champion as a Stanford sophomore and a golf phenom ever since he sat in a high chair at the age of six months and watched his father, Earl, hit golf balls into a net in their Cypress, California, home. But his mother, Kultida, established his value system.

"When Tiger was just a toddler," Earl Woods recalled in his book, *Training a Tiger*, "Tida wrote the addition and multiplication tables on three-by-five-inch cards, and he would practice them over and over every day. He started with addition and later advanced to multiplication as he got older. His reward was an afternoon on the practice range with me. Tida established irrevocably that education had a priority over golf."

Tiger's first name is Eldrick, but his father nicknamed him after a legendary Vietnamese colonel, Nguyen ("Tiger") Phong.

By the age of three, Tiger was so proficient at golf that he appeared on *The Mike Douglas Show*, putting with Bob Hope. At four, he arrived at the Heartwell Golf Park, a municipal 18-hole par-3 course in Long Beach, California, after several of Earl's friends had recommended Rudy Duran, the teaching pro there.

"Tiger took out his driver and began hitting ropes, straight shots down the middle about ninety yards," Duran has said. "He had a full backswing even then. He looked like a shrunken Jack Nicklaus."

Tiger was soon fitted for a custom set of junior clubs that included what would become his favorite, a 1-iron, and Duran established what he called "Tiger par." On a 150-yard hole, Tiger's 90-yard drive, 60-yard 5-iron, and 2 putts for 4 was par.

"I wanted to get him accustomed to trying to shoot a good score," Duran recalled. "The first time he broke Tiger par was just after his fifth birthday when he shot eight under."

At ages eight and nine, Tiger won the first two of his six Optimist International Junior World titles. At age ten, he was hitting 200-yard drives, but when Duran moved away to another job, Tiger's father took him to another tutor, John Anselmo, the pro at the Meadowlark course in Huntington Beach, California.

"Tiger played every chance he got and loved to practice," Anselmo remembered. "He knew how to practice, not just beat balls on the range. If he had a bad round in the wind, he'd say, 'I need to know how to hit knockdown shots.' I'd show him what to do, he'd work on it for a while, and he had it."

At fifteen, he won the 1991 U.S. Junior Amateur, the start of his record streak of three U.S. Junior Amateurs and three U.S. Amateurs.

In the 1996 U.S. Amateur final, Tiger was 2 down with 3 holes to play against Steve Scott, but he rallied to square the match on the 36th hole, then won on the 2nd extra hole. Two days later, he announced he was turning pro as no other golfer ever had, signing a $40 million deal with Nike sports apparel and a $20 million deal with Titleist golf equipment.

Tiger Woods celebrates a putt en route to his third consecutive U.S. Amateur title in 1996.

"I'm just hoping to win enough money in the year's last seven tournaments," he said, "so I qualify for the 1997 PGA Tour."

To get his PGA Tour card, Tiger figured he needed to earn about $150,000 to finish in the year's top 125 money winners. But he did what no other rookie had ever done. He won two tournaments, the Las Vegas Invitational and the Disney/Oldsmobile Classic, and earned $790,594 to finish 25th on the money list.

In his first 1997 tournament, the Mercedes Championship at La Costa near San Diego, he won again, this time in a playoff with Tom Lehman, spinning a 6-iron to within 6 inches of the cup on the 188-yard 7th hole after Lehman had splashed his 6-iron into a pond.

He also would win the GTE Byron Nelson Classic and the Motorola Western Open, but his Masters victory would justify all the hype, all his multi-million-dollar contracts, and all the hours his father spent with him on the golf course as a youngster. As he walked off the 18th green as the winner, he all but disappeared into his father's arms.

"It's an understanding that he and I have," Earl Woods said later. "I want him, when he brings it to closure, I want to have him in my arms. I told him right then, let it go. He knows that all the heartbreak and effort and strain and tension is over, that he's safe in Dad's arms."

But with a 9-stroke lead on Saturday night before that final round, Tiger had appeared safe enough. Colin Montgomerie, the European Ryder Cupper, had just shot 74 while paired with Tiger, who shot 65. Montgomerie knew that this kid was as good as advertised, if not even better.

"I have a brief comment," Montgomerie said in the media center. "We're all human beings here, but there is no chance humanly

Tiger Woods hugs his father, Earl, at the 1997 Masters.

possible that Tiger Woods is going to lose this golf tournament. No way. Nick Faldo's not lying second, for a start, and Tiger Woods is not Greg Norman."

On Saturday night at the Masters the year before, Norman, the Australian in the akubra hat, had a 6-stroke lead. Most people thought he would win going away, but Faldo hadn't surrendered. Even though Faldo was 5 strokes behind Norman, the precise Englishman knew, as he said that Saturday night, that "anything can happen" after they teed off together in Sunday's final pairing.

"Put a little pressure on him," Faldo said. "You never know."

Sunday had seldom been Norman's best day. Over his career, he had failed to win four other major tournaments after holding the 54-hole lead and failed to win a fifth after being the third-round co-leader. And on Sunday at the 1996 Masters, he failed again. He soared to a 78 while Faldo stormed to a 67, an 11-stroke swing that enabled Faldo to win by 5 strokes.

With his third Masters to accompany his three British Open championships, Faldo had been the world's most dominant golfer for a decade while Norman had been the world's most disappointed golfer, despite two British Open titles and more than $10 million in PGA Tour earnings.

Norman arrived from Australia at the 1981 Masters with tee shots that resembled jet fighters taking off. Then twenty-six, he had grown up near the Great Barrier Reef, where he remembered shooting sharks, prompting his instant nickname: the Great White Shark. He had won fourteen tournaments in Australia, Asia, and Europe, and he would win twelve more on those continents before winning a PGA Tour event, the 1994 Kemper Open at Congressional outside Washington, D.C.

In 1986, he won his first major, the British Open at Turnberry, with a record 63 in the second round, but he would be remembered more for the three majors he didn't win that year.

In the Masters, which Jack Nicklaus won with a 65 in the final round, Norman held the 54-hole lead but shot 70 in the final round for 280, tying Tom Kite for second. In the U.S. Open at Shinnecock Hills, he again had the 54-hole lead but shot 75 for 285, 6 strokes behind the forty-three-year-old champion, Raymond Floyd. In the PGA Championship at Inverness in Toledo, Ohio, he again had the 54-hole lead but shot 76, losing by 2 when Bob Tway holed a sand-wedge from a bunker at the final green.

In a sense, Norman was close to a Grand Slam of the four majors in 1986, yet finished far away from it. In the following years, it seemed to be the story of his life in the majors.

In the 1987 Masters, Norman waited on the 11th green, his ball about 30 feet from the cup on this 2nd sudden-death playoff hole, as Larry Mize addressed a tricky chip shot off the green, about 140 feet from the cup. But like a lightning bolt out of a blue sky, Mize's chip rolled across the green and into the hole. Birdie. Norman missed his birdie putt. Second again.

Norman won the 1993 British Open at Royal St. George's, then had the 54-hole lead in that year's PGA Championship at Inverness, but lost a sudden-death playoff to Paul Azinger on the 2nd hole. And in the 1995 U.S. Open at Shinnecock Hills, he again had the 54-hole lead but shot 73 in the final round, finishing 2 strokes behind Corey Pavin.

With seventy tournament victories around the world and numerous multimillion-dollar endorsement contracts, Norman was living in a Hobe Sound, Florida, mansion with his own jet, two helicopters, a yacht, and half a dozen cars before he stormed to a record-tying 63 in the first round of the 1996 Masters. But after his 78 in the final round, he was second again. Upon putting out on

For all the tournaments Greg Norman won, he'll always be remembered for the 1996 Masters that got away.

Nick Faldo raises his arms in victory—his third Masters title.

the final green, Faldo hugged him.

"I don't know what to say," Faldo told him. "I just want to give you a hug."

Other pros knew what to say. According to Faldo's European Ryder Cup teammate, Colin Montgomerie, "This was the one guy Greg didn't want in his rearview mirror. The one guy Greg didn't want playing with him was the guy he had." Faldo is considered to be one of golf's best thinkers and one of its best pressure players.

"I was in control, which is the big thrill," he said later of his 5-under-par 67 that won the Masters. "I hit all the shots where I intended to hit them on the day it had to be done."

Faldo's round was virtually perfect. He missed only one green, he had 13 putts under 20 feet, and he had only one downhill putt on greens where it is best to be putting from below the cup. But to those who know him and had seen him win thirty-seven times around the world up to then, his victory wasn't that surprising.

"Nick is a very intimidating character on the golf course," Montgomerie explained. "That's possibly why he's won six majors. He won one outright, the 1990 British Open. The other five have been because of who he is, the aura that he has, and because a few people have folded in his presence coming in."

That aura was apparent in Faldo's comeback victory over Curtis Strange at Oak Hill in the 1995 Ryder Cup's decisive singles match. Two down with 3 holes to play, Faldo won all 3, sinking an 8-foot putt on the final green that enhanced his deserved reputation at the time as the world's best golfer.

"Nick just loves the fact that he is the best," his golf guru, David Leadbetter, said in 1992. "He is always conscious of not letting up, always totally focused on getting that little bit better."

Growing up in England, Faldo had turned to golf after watching Jack Nicklaus overtake Charles Coody in the 1971 Masters. Early in his career, he let a few tournaments get away, prompting the British media to dub him Nick Foldo. But once he matured as a golfer, his opponents were the ones who folded. In 1995, he decided to play the PGA Tour in America full-time.

"The biggest reason for going to the States," he said, "was to work on my game so I could win more majors."

In the 1996 Masters, Faldo did just that, but in 1997, as if passing golf's torch, he held the Masters green jacket for Tiger Woods to put on as the new winner. Suddenly, this twenty-one-year-old phenom was being touted as the successor to Bobby Jones, Ben Hogan, and Jack Nicklaus as the world's best golfer in his era, but he knew it would take years to justify those predictions.

"People can say all kinds of things about me and Jack Nicklaus and make me into whatever," Tiger Woods said. "But it comes down to one thing. I've still got to hit the shot. Me. Alone. That's what I must never forget."

AS THE FIRST UNITED STATES WOMAN GOLFER TO WIN the British Ladies Amateur championship in 1947, Babe Zaharias stunned the English galleries with her towering tee shots. After the trophy presentation, she was asked the secret of her power.

"I just loosen my girdle," she said, "and let the ball have it."

This was an athlete. As eighteen-year-old Mildred ("Babe") Didrikson at the 1932 Olympics in Los Angeles, she had won gold medals in the javelin and the high hurdles, and a silver medal in the high jump. As a Texas schoolgirl, she had been the equivalent of an All-America basketball player.

Shortly after the Olympics, she began playing golf but didn't devote herself to it seriously until after World War II. In 1946, she won the U.S. Women's Amateur with an 11 and 9 rout in the final during a winning streak of fifteen matches.

Turning pro for a $300,000 contract to do golf movies in Hollywood, she won the U.S. Women's Open in 1949 and 1950 and, after surgery for rectal cancer, won it again in 1954 by a record 12 strokes. She died two years later at age forty-two. But her legacy was her founding in 1950, along with Patty Berg, Louise Suggs, and Betty Jameson, the Ladies Professional Golfers Association (LPGA) tour that has evolved into the stage for the world's best golfers, notably Mickey Wright and Nancy Lopez.

"Women wanted a tour like the men had," Berg said. "The Babe gave us the credibility we needed."

Berg, Suggs, and Jameson also provided credibility. Berg, who had been a Marine lieutenant during World War II, won fifty-seven tournaments, including the inaugural U.S. Women's Open in 1946. Suggs won fifty tournaments, including two Opens, and Jameson won ten, including the 1947 Open.

But when the Babe loosened her girdle, more people started paying attention to women's golf. Her accomplishments were accepted as those of an Olympic and All-America athlete.

Babe Zaharias with her U.S. Women's Open trophy

Even so, women's golf has, often unfairly, taken a backseat to men's golf, if only because women golfers seldom hit the ball as far. Yardage on holes from the women's tees was also shorter than that from the men's tees. In general, women golfers seldom received the headlines and the television coverage accorded men.

But ever since Mary, Queen of Scots, played the Old Course at St. Andrews centuries ago, golf has offered women an opportunity that few other sports do—being able to beat a man. At whatever golf course the game is played around the world, the best female golfers there often shoot better scores than many of the male golfers. But in tournament play on the LPGA tour or at the national, state, or local amateur level, women usually compete only against other women.

Although the yardage length of each hole and each course is usually slightly shorter from the women's tees than from the men's tees, and the overall women's par might be 73 or 74 instead of the men's par of 72, women play basically the same course as men.

In the inaugural Wendy's Three-Tour Challenge in 1992 at New Albany Country Club in Columbus, Ohio, the LPGA team of Nancy Lopez, Dottie Pepper, and Patty Sheehan defeated the Senior PGA Tour trio of Jack Nicklaus, Juan ("Chi Chi") Rodriguez, and Larry Laoretti, and the PGA Tour threesome of Raymond Floyd, Tom Kite, and Fred Couples.

In golf, the swing's the thing, not the gender. Joyce Wethered was the first woman to prove that. Of the twelve British ladies tournaments that the tall, slender Englishwoman entered from 1920 through 1929, she won nine. Known as Lady Heathcote Amory after her marriage, she had a simple explanation for her success.

"Golf," she said, "is just one good shot after another."

But that one good shot after another is also the result of other factors, particularly concentration on each shot. During one tournament, everybody in Wethered's gallery heard a train rumble by. But when she was asked if the train had bothered her, she was surprised.

"What train?" she asked.

That's concentration. And that, along with one of the sweetest swings in golf, is why Wethered's contemporaries, notably Bobby Jones, considered this British champion to be the best woman golfer of their time.

"I have not played with anyone, man or woman, amateur or professional," Jones said, "who made me feel so utterly outclassed."

In that same era, before the LPGA was formed, Glenna Collett Vare dominated United States women's golf with a record six U.S. Women's Amateur titles. Out of Providence, Rhode Island, she had been a swimmer and a diver as well as a tennis and a baseball player until she was inspired to play golf after watching Alexa Stirling, a three-time U.S. Women's Amateur champion.

Glenna Collett Vare

"Wethered and Vare have to be judged on what they did as amateurs," Gene Sarazen once said, "but they were still the best women golfers I've ever seen."

Wethered and Vare were opponents in the inaugural Curtis Cup matches in 1932 between women amateur golfers from the United States and from Great Britain and Ireland. Formally known as The Women's International Cup, the trophy was officially presented by the Curtis sisters, Margaret and Harriott, who had won the U.S. Women's Amateur four times between them.

"To stimulate friendly rivalry,"

its inscription read, "among the women golfers of many lands."

Vare was on that victorious first U.S. Curtis Cup team, along with Maureen Orcutt, Virginia Van Wie, Helen Hicks, Opal Hill, Dorothy Higbie, and Leona Pressler Cheney. Through 1996, the U.S. women amateurs held a 20–6–3 edge in the biennial matches, and Carol Semple Thompson had been a team member a record nine times with a record fifteen victories.

But with the growth of the LPGA tour, many of the best United States women golfers preferred to turn pro rather than remain amateurs, notably Mickey Wright, Kathy Whitworth, and Betsy Rawls.

In assessing Wright's "perfect swing," which helped her win eighty-two tournaments on the LPGA tour, including four U.S. Women's Opens and four LPGA Championships, golf historians fondly remember her 69–72 on the 1961 Open's final day at Baltusrol's Lower course. But she remembered the putts she missed.

"I two-putted everything," the Texan said, alluding to her par 72 in the afternoon after having made 6 birdies in her morning round. "I remember being upset at myself for not putting better after having played such a good round."

Wright was the only one upset. Everybody else at Baltusrol that day was in awe of how she had rallied to win by 6 strokes after having been 4 strokes behind, following an inexplicable 80 in the second round. But winning was what she did best. In 1963, she won thirteen LPGA events, a one-year record not likely to be broken. After 1969, Wright no longer played regularly because of various ailments, but in 1997 the LPGA still described her as "perhaps the greatest player" in its history.

Two of Wright's contemporaries, Kathy Whitworth and Betsy Rawls, would also establish themselves among history's best.

Whitworth, considered a great putter, won an LPGA-record eighty-eight tournaments and seven Vare Trophies for the best scoring average. She was also the leading money winner eight times. Rawls won fifty-five tournaments, including four U.S.

Mickey Wright

Women's Opens (a record shared with Wright), and two LPGA Championships. One of Rawls's Open victories occurred in 1957 at Winged Foot's East course in Mamaroneck, New York, when Jackie Pung, the apparent winner, was disqualified.

Pung's total score was correct, but she had signed a scorecard on which her fellow competitor and marker had mistakenly put down a 5 on the 4th hole rather than the 6 that Pung had made. One of golf's rules is that a golfer must sign a correct scorecard. If it's not correct, the golfer is disqualified. When Pung was disqualified, the Winged Foot members collected some $3,000 for her, about $1,200 more than the first-prize money.

Nancy Lopez

In 1969, as Mickey Wright's career was coming to an end, the career of a little girl in Roswell, New Mexico, was beginning to blossom.

Nancy Lopez won the New Mexico Women's Amateur that year, but her triumph wasn't as startling as the age at which she won. She was twelve. That's still a national record for the youngest women's state amateur champion. And she's been winning ever since, even while raising three daughters—Ashley Marie, Errin Shea, and Torri Heather.

"I could have just played golf and never had any children at all," she has said. "But then you grow old and risk ending up alone. To someday have grandchildren, being a parent, experiencing family—that's special to me."

Lopez has been special to golf. In 1978, her first full year on the LPGA tour, she won nine events, five in a row. Through 1997, she had won forty-eight tour events, including three LPGA Championships and the 1981 Colgate Dinah Shore.

JoAnne Carner isn't far behind, with forty-two victories, including two U.S. Women's Opens. She is the only Open champion to have won the U.S. Girls Junior and the U.S. Women's Amateur. Known as The Great Gundy (Gunderson was her maiden name) before she turned pro at age thirty, she won five U.S. Women's Amateurs. Her eight USGA titles are the most for a woman and only one behind Bobby Jones's record nine.

Win or lose, Carner's determined but relaxed style always gave her galleries the impression that she was having fun.

"I love it," she once said in her gravelly voice. "I was born a competitor, and that's what I've loved to do."

Lopez and Carner soon joined the LPGA Hall of Fame, perhaps the most exclusive pantheon in sports. To enter the Hall, a golfer must win thirty official events, including two major championships, or thirty-five official events with one major championship, or forty official events exclusive of any majors. The LPGA's pioneer women (Zaharias, Berg, Suggs, and Jameson) are also there, along with Sandra Haynie, Carol Mann, Pat Bradley, Patty Sheehan, and Betsy King.

Bradley earned over $5 million on the LPGA tour while winning six major titles, including the 1981 U.S. Women's Open and the 1986 LPGA Championship. Sheehan won the U.S. Women's Open twice, the LPGA Championship three times. King won the 1989 U.S. Women's Open and the 1992 LPGA Championship, as well as the 1987 and 1990 Dinah Shore.

More and more, however, the long domination of the LPGA tour by the American women was being threatened by an invasion of

Laura Davies

European talent, notably Laura Davies of England and Annika Sorenstam of Sweden. The emergence of the European women created in 1990 the biennial Solheim Cup matches, the United States against Europe in a women's version of the men's Ryder Cup matches. The cup was named for Karsten Solheim, founder of the Karsten Manufacturing Corporation that produced Ping clubs.

In winning the 1987 U.S. Women's Open at the Plainfield (New Jersey) Country Club, Davies, a newcomer who had not even qualified for the LPGA tour at the time, had stunned golf observers with her length off the tee.

During the summer of 1995, Davies's measured drives were averaging 269.3 yards—farther than Nick Faldo, Tom Lehman, and Phil Mickelson, among dozens of others, were averaging on the PGA Tour, farther than Jack Nicklaus and Arnold Palmer were averaging on the Senior PGA Tour. Taller and stronger than most women golfers at 5–10 and 200 pounds, she wasn't surprised.

"I take dead aim down the

middle and dead aim at the pin," Davies often said. "I hate laying up. I hate leaving putts short. It's just all-out attack."

Another European, Annika Sorenstam, who grew up in Stockholm, Sweden, soon was challenging Davies for supremacy among the world's women golfers. In 1995, she was the leading money winner on both the American and European tours. That same year, she won the U.S. Women's Open at the Broadmoor in Colorado Springs. In 1996, while winning her second consecutive Vare Trophy for the LPGA's lowest scoring average, she retained the U.S. Women's Open title at Pine Needles in Pinehurst, North Carolina.

"To do this again," she said. "I'm out of words."

But she was not out of the ordinary. Annika Sorenstam is merely the latest in a long line of women who play golf better than most men.

Annika Sorenstam with the 1996 U.S. Women's Open trophy

part **Two**

Pine Valley's
18th green

Euphoria and Disaster

EVER SINCE 1985, PINE VALLEY, A SANDY TORTURE chamber in the pine trees of southern New Jersey, across the Delaware River from Philadelphia, has been number one in "America's 100 Greatest Golf Courses," as ranked biannually by *Golf Digest* magazine.

And deservedly so.

No golf course is more tormenting not only for the quality golfer but also, even more so, for the duffer. One day on its 14th hole, a par 3 of 185 yards from the back tee with water in front of the green and behind it, a relatively decent golfer who shall go unnamed shot…well, start counting.

His tee shot landed on the green but skipped into the water beyond. Splash.

Upon hitting his 3rd shot from the drop area on the other side of the water, this man, who has been described as "the president of a famous golf club," suddenly caught a serious case of the shanks, a malady that caused the ball to veer uncontrollably to the right into the water. Again and again and again.

Eventually, and still counting, he got a ball on the green with his 40th stroke, then 3-putted for a 43, a mere 40 over par on that one hole.

But not all Pine Valley stories have such an unhappy ending. One of its more celebrated members, Woodie Platt, who won the Philadelphia Amateur seven times between 1920 and 1942, is proof of that, as well as proof that golf is not always a humbling game.

In a casual round one day, he opened with a birdie 3 on the 427-yard 1st hole, a dogleg right. Not that unusual.

After a solid drive on the 367-yard 2nd, he lofted a 7-iron over the yawning bunkers onto the elevated green, and his ball rolled into the cup. Eagle 2.

On the 185-yard 3rd, he had a hole in one.

After another solid drive on the 461-yard 4th, he drilled a 4-wood onto the green, then sank a 30-foot putt. Birdie 3.

Over the first four holes of this most difficult of courses, he had needed only 9 strokes. He was 6 under par.

But rather than stroll over to the tee of the 226-yard 5th hole, he chose to disappear into the nearby Pine Valley clubhouse.

Never to reappear. At least not that day.

Woodie Platt knew he couldn't possibly continue such a scoring streak, that he could only do worse, that there was no need to spoil the historic value of his 3-2-1-3 start on one of America's, if not the world's, most demanding golf courses.

It was his day, but he chose not to resume it.

Such extremes, a 43 on one hole and a 9 for the first four holes, are what golf is all about. Disaster for some. Euphoria for others. That's the nature of golf where, except for overall yardage, no two holes anywhere in the world are exactly alike any more than two golfers are exactly alike.

That's also the charm of golf. That's why people want to play different courses, why they travel to famous courses.

The most famous is the Old Course at St. Andrews, the golf shrine that brings golf pilgrims to the old gray university town of St. Andrews on Scotland's eastern coast. It's known as the home of golf, the home of the first golf course along the Scottish linksland, the strips of treeless wilderness that remained when the seas receded after the last Ice Age.

At first glance, the Old Course at St. Andrews, like other British links courses near the sea, resembles a moonscape. Some people don't like it, but that's because they don't understand it.

Jack Nicklaus, who won the 1978 British Open on the Old Course, has called it "my favorite place on earth to play golf." Bobby Jones, who as an impetuous nineteen-year-old tore up his scorecard and stalked off after a 6 on the par-3 11th hole during the 1921 British Open, also came to appreciate it. On his induction years later as an honorary burgess of St. Andrews, he explained his feelings for the Old Course.

"The more I studied the Old Course, the more I loved it, and the more I loved it, the more I studied it," he said. "I came to feel that it was for me the most favorable meeting ground possible for an important contest. I felt that my knowledge of the course enabled me to play it with patience and restraint until she might exact her toll from my adversary, who might treat her with less respect and under-standing."

Part of the Old Course's attraction is that it's a public course, meaning anyone can play it. Call a St. Andrews phone number, put your name into the daily lottery (what the Scots call the ballot), and hope you draw a tee time for the next day (except for Sunday, when the Old Course is closed). If your name is drawn, it's posted with your tee time. Arrive at least fifteen minutes early, pay the greens fee to the starter, and tee off.

If you're smart, you'll have hired a caddie, the older the better. Without a caddie, you won't know the line off the tee, you won't know the best line to the green, and you won't know the line of your putt.

Most importantly, a caddie will warn you about the bunkers you must avoid on the Old Course if you are to score decently. Especially the deep pot bunker next to the green on the 461-yard 17th, one of the world's most difficult holes. It's known as the Road Hole because an old road is behind the green. Beyond the road is an old stone wall.

Every so often, a golfer's ball will come to rest on the road or against that wall.

That deep greenside bunker can be even more damaging to your score. Tommy Nakajima will attest to that.

In the 1978 British Open's third round, the Japanese pro, who would become a periodic contender on the PGA Tour, was safely on the green in 2, putting for a birdie that would put him among the leaders. But when he putted, his ball curled down a slope into the deep pot bunker. So deep that a golfer seems to disappear in it. Only the flying sand is seen. Once, twice, three times, the sand flew, but Nakajima's ball failed to emerge. On his fourth blast, his ball finally popped onto the green. He 2-putted for a 9.

Ever since then, that deep pot bunker has been known as The Sands of Nakajima.

All over Great Britain (Scotland, England, Wales) and Ireland, deep bunkers swallow golf balls. Deep bunkers, along with gorse (a prickly green shrub), high brown grass, narrow creeks (known as burns), and only a few small trees make British and Irish links courses unlike those anywhere else in the world.

In the United States, a few links courses exist, notably Shinnecock Hills in Southampton, New York, at the eastern end of Long Island where the topography is somewhat similar to that of British linksland. Constructed in 1891 with the help of one hundred fifty workers from the nearby Shinnecock Indian reservation (its grounds crew is still dominated by Shinnecocks), it was the site of the second U.S. Open in 1896. Nearly a century later, as the host of the 1986 U.S. Open and the centennial 1995 U.S. Open, it justified its reputation as one of America's best courses.

"The wind is what makes Shinnecock Hills," its club pro, Don McDougald, has said. "During the four days of the 1986 Open, the wind blew from the north on Thursday, from the south on Friday, from the west on Saturday, from the east on Sunday. The pros had to play four different courses."

In general, American courses have a much different look from that of British courses. On American courses, the bunkers are wider and longer but seldom deep. The fairways are greener and softer, the grass in the rough relatively short and thin. The danger is in the ponds, wide streams, and forests of tall trees that await a sliced or hooked shot.

At Augusta National, the annual site of the Masters tournament in Georgia, the water holes on the back 9 invariably affect the outcome. Especially the 12th hole—a deceptively difficult par 3 of 155 yards over Rae's Creek to a narrow green.

Jack Nicklaus, who has won the Masters a record six times, has called the 12th "the most demanding tournament hole in the

Shinnecock Hills' 18th green

In the shadows of towering pine trees, Augusta National is center stage for the Masters each year. Greg Norman (far right) slumps in disappointment as his ball slides past the pin on the 15th green in 1995's final round.

world." Over the years, he has hit anywhere from a 4-iron to a 9-iron off the tee, depending on the strength of the wind blowing above the creek through the gap in the pine trees.

At Augusta, the 12th hole is the middle hole of what is known as Amen Corner—the par-4 downhill 465-yard 11th with a pond to the left of the green, the treacherous 12th, and the par-5 dogleg left 485-yard 13th that tempts the golfer who has hit a big drive to risk carrying a watery ditch.

Unlike other tournament courses, Augusta National has virtually no rough. Its guardians of par are its water holes, its cathedral-like pine trees, and its slick undulating greens.

"To win the Masters," Tom Watson has said, "you must hit your approach shots to the correct areas of the green, depending on where the cup has been cut that day. If your ball is relatively close to the hole, you have a chance for a birdie. But if you're too far away, you're likely to three-putt."

During the 1996 Masters, Watson, a two-time winner there, needed 5 putts at the sloping 16th green after his 6-iron tee shot rolled to a stop about 60 feet below the cup.

"I went from sixty below," he said later, meaning the distance in feet, "to six above, to forty below, to four above, to two below, then I made that one. I never remember five-putting."

The fastest greens in American golf (and the most bedeviling bunker) are at Oakmont in the foothills of the Allegheny Mountains near Pittsburgh. Designed in 1903 by Henry Fownes, Oakmont once had more than 350 bunkers. About half no longer exist, but the

Augusta National's 13th green

"church pews" do. Situated between the 3rd and 4th fairways, this bunker is about 60 yards long and 40 yards wide with seven separate grassy ridges in the sand. As for the greens there, it's not unusual for a golfer to putt his ball off the green.

"These greens are so slick," Lew Worsham, the longtime Oakmont pro, once said, "nobody I know uses any kind of a putter except a blade. If you used a mallet-head putter, that would be like getting a back rub with a sledgehammer."

For all the speed of the Oakmont greens, Johnny Miller, now a television golf analyst, won the 1973 U.S. Open there with a 9-under-par 63 in the final round, an Open record that Jack Nicklaus and Tom Weiskopf tied in the first round of the 1980 Open at Baltusrol. Miller did it on Sunday with the Open at stake. With 9 birdies, 9 pars. But as historic as Oakmont was for Miller, he, like so many others, considers Pebble Beach to be his favorite course.

"It's the most beautiful place in the world, like it was made in heaven," Miller once said, alluding to the Monterey Peninsula on the northern California coast. "I can't think of another course I enjoy as much as Pebble Beach."

Like St. Andrews, Pebble Beach is a public course in the sense that it's a resort course. If you're staying at the Lodge at Pebble Beach or if you're anywhere near the Monterey Peninsula, you can get a tee time—at a price. By late 1997, the cost for a nonguest at the Lodge was $295 plus $25 for a cart ($45 plus tip for a caddie). Lodge guests got a free cart.

Jack Nicklaus won the U.S. Open there in 1972, Tom Watson won it there in 1982, and Tom Kite won it there in 1992, but no matter what you shoot, the views are always spectacular.

Pebble Beach is known for its stretch of punishing par-4 cliffside holes midway through the round—the 431-yard 8th with a 2nd shot over a chasm where Carmel Bay's surf can be heard crashing against the rocks, the 464-yard 9th down a fairway that tumbles from left to right to a green near the cliffs, the 426-yard 10th, where a pushed

Oakmont's devilish "church pews" bunkers

tee shot can land on the beach below the cliffs that also threaten the 2nd shot.

Up the road is Cypress Point, which many consider the most naturally beautiful course in the world with the most naturally beautiful hole in the world, its 233-yard 16th, a par 3 over white-capped waves to a green on a rockbound peninsula.

For more than forty years, Cypress Point was one of the three courses used for what was once known as the Bing Crosby National Pro-Am, with Pebble Beach one of the other two courses. In the 1959 Crosby, an amateur named Hans Merrell took a 19 at the 16th, but Crosby, the crooner and movie star, was among the few ever to ace the 16th. The 16th is merely the most dazzling hole on a dazzling course where sea lions can be heard barking while deer graze on an empty fairway.

"Pebble Beach has six great holes, all those that lie on the coast-line," Julius Boros, a two-time U.S. Open champion, once said. "Cypress Point has eighteen great holes, whether they lie on the coast or not."

Like anything else in life, the beauty of golf courses is in the eye of the beholder. Johnny Miller thinks Pebble Beach is the most beautiful, but others prefer Cypress Point or Oakmont or Augusta National or Shinnecock Hills or St. Andrews or Pine Valley or one of dozens of others, maybe Winged Foot or Oakland Hills or Baltusrol or Oak Hill or Pinehurst No. 2 or Olympic or Congressional or Quaker Ridge or Seminole or the National Golf Links of America or The Country Club or Medinah or Merion or Riviera or Carnoustie or Royal St. George's or Turnberry or Royal Troon or Prestwick or Muirfield or Valderrama or Royal Melbourne or Banff. Or some other course.

You might consider your favorite course to be the most beautiful you've ever seen. And if you do, then it is.

ARCHITECTS OF GRASS, SAND, AND WATER

WHEN THE 1954 U.S. OPEN WAS AWARDED TO THE Baltusrol Golf Club's Lower course, the 120-yard 4th hole was deemed too easy. Just a little wedge shot over a pond. Not tough enough for Ben Hogan, Sam Snead, and the other touring pros who would be playing in the U.S. Open. So golf's most renowned architect of that era, Robert Trent Jones, was hired to toughen that hole.

He lengthened it to 192 yards from the back tee. He enlarged the green, bringing it down to the very edge of the pond.

Somewhat predictably, some Baltusrol members now considered the hole to be too difficult. Maybe not for the pros who would be playing in the U.S. Open, but too difficult for them, even from the 165-yard middle tee. Too many golf balls were splashing into the pond.

"It's an unfair hole," they griped.

Jones agreed to audition the hole's fairness. At an appointed hour, the members were invited to watch him play the hole along with Johnny Farrell, the Baltusrol pro who had won the 1928 U.S. Open in a playoff with Bobby Jones, and two Baltusrol members (the club president and the chairman of its U.S. Open committee).

Hitting from the 165-yard markers, Farrell and the two members each put their golf balls on the green.

Jones, who had once been a top golfer in the Rochester, New York, area good enough to be the low amateur in the 1927 Canadian Open, was nearing his forty-eighth birthday. But with a smooth swing of his 4-iron, his golf ball soared over the pond, landed on the green, and rolled into the cup. Hole in one.

**Baltusrol's
4th green**

"Gentlemen," Jones said, turning to the assembled Baltusrol members, "the hole is fair. Eminently fair."

With that hole in one, Jones proved to have been eminently correct in his redesign of Baltusrol's 4th hole, which, incidentally, Tom Watson would ace in the first round of the 1980 U.S. Open. But that's what good golf architects do. They are golf's sculptors. Just as a sculptor takes a chunk of marble and sculpts it into a statue, a golf architect takes a tract of land and shapes it into a golf course.

In the evolution of golf in America, architects such as Donald Ross, Alister MacKenzie, and Albert W. Tillinghast dominated the early years of the twentieth century, then Robert Trent Jones (known as Trent Jones) stood alone in his era before the emergence, in the last quarter of the century, of his two sons, Rees Jones and Robert Trent Jones, Jr., along with Tom Fazio, Pete Dye, and Jack Nicklaus.

"Golf architecture," Trent Jones has said, "is a form of attack and counterattack. It offers a golfer his personal challenge of combat. He attacks the course and par. The architect creates fair pitfalls to defend par's easy conquest. The architect calls on his ingenuity to create a hole that will reward only achievement. Every hole should be a hard par and an easy bogey. The shattering of par without a proper challenge is a fraud."

Throughout the world, Trent Jones has defended par more than any other architect.

He designed more than three hundred fifty courses in forty-five states and twenty-three foreign countries, notably Valderrama in Spain, the site of the 1997 Ryder Cup matches. He also redesigned more than one hundred fifty other courses, including six U.S. Open sites. He collaborated with Bobby Jones in remodeling Augusta National's 11th and 16th holes, and in designing the Peachtree Golf Club in Atlanta. He installed a putting green on the White House lawn for President Dwight Eisenhower. His clients included the Aga Khan and King Hassan II of Morocco, but he didn't just deal with royalty or wealthy clubs and resorts. When he was nearing his eighty-seventh birthday, he designed eighteen public courses in seven Alabama locales. Known as the Robert Trent Jones Golf Trail, they opened in 1993.

"The sun," he proudly said, "never sets on a Robert Trent Jones golf course."

His reputation as a defender of par developed when he was hired to toughen Oakland Hills, near Detroit, for the 1951 U.S. Open. The touring pros griped that the course was now too difficult, even for them. In the opening round, Ben Hogan shot a 6-over-par 76, but he rallied to win his third of four U.S. Open titles with his memorable 3-under-par 67 in the final round. Hogan's 67 and Clayton Haefner's final-round 69 were the only under-par scores all week. After the trophy presentation, Hogan happened to see Trent Jones's wife, Ione.

"If your husband," Hogan said, "had to play this course for a living, he'd be on the bread line."

When Mrs. Jones told her husband what Hogan had said about the Oakland Hills course, Trent Jones just chuckled.

"I'm the one person the pros like to complain about," he often said. "I make them play par."

Trent Jones's courses offer multiple routes and risks. He used dogleg holes, huge bunkers, and water hazards that force golfers, no matter what their level of skill, to make choices. Go for the difficult par, accept the easy bogey. He also popularized long tees, which provide various course lengths for golfers with various handicaps.

Growing up in East Rochester, New York, Trent Jones was inspired to study surveying, agronomy, and landscaping at Cornell University after conversations with Donald Ross when the legendary Scottish architect was building Oak Hill in 1926. At the time, Ross was America's most popular golf architect, having settled in Pinehurst, North Carolina.

"Sand is the ideal soil for a golf course," Ross often said. "At Pinehurst, we have an especially suitable sand soil. We are able to handle the greens and approaches in ways that would otherwise not be possible, such as the creation of hollows and contouring that would present impossible drainage problems in anything but a natural sandy soil."

While stressing the value of chipping and putting, Ross designed over four hundred courses, including Oakland Hills and five at Pinehurst, then and now one of America's most popular golf areas. His masterpiece is Pinehurst No. 2, with its crowned greens, the site of the 1999 U.S. Open.

"Make each hole present a different problem," he once wrote. "So arrange it that every stroke must be made with a full concentration and attention necessary to good golf. Build each hole in such a manner that it wastes none of the ground and takes advantage of every possibility. A course that continually offers problems—one with fight in it, if you please—is the one that keeps the players keen for the game. It will be difficult to negotiate some holes, but that is what golf is for. It is a mental test, an eye test. The hazards and bunkers are placed so as to force a man to use judgment and to exercise mental control in making the correct shot."

For any golfer who might complain about the location of a bunker, whether near a fairway or a green, Ross enjoyed countering with his philosophy.

"There is no such thing as a misplaced bunker," he said. "Regardless of where a bunker may be, it is the business of the player to avoid it."

During Ross's career, Albert W. Tillinghast, who grew up in Philadelphia but made pilgrimages to St. Andrews to take golf lessons from Old Tom Morris, also was designing some of America's best courses —Winged Foot's West and East courses as well as neighboring Quaker Ridge, the San Francisco Golf Club, Baltusrol's Lower course, and Bethpage's Black course on Long Island, which in 2002 will be the first publicly owned U.S. Open site in the championship's history.

A. W. Tillinghast

"Golf holes are like men," the architect known as Tillie often said. "All rather similar from foot to neck, but with the greens showing the same varying characters as human faces."

Tillinghast's undulating roller-coaster greens bedevil golfers. On the first green of Winged Foot's West course in the 1974 U.S. Open, Jack Nicklaus stroked a 20-foot birdie putt, but when his ball slid off a ridge, he suddenly was putting for par from 25 feet below the cup.

"Nothing can supply a green with more character than bold undulations," Tillinghast said. "A ball will kick in safely if properly played, or else be deflected considerably if slightly off line. Therefore, the correct line of play is not always straight to the pin."

From tee to green, the correct line of play is also not always straight to the pin. At Augusta National, for example, five holes—the 2nd, 5th, 9th, 10th, and 13th—are dogleg holes, as designed by its coarchitects, Bobby Jones and Alister MacKenzie.

"An astonishing amount of golf—that is, good golf—is played between the ears," Jones wrote in his foreword to MacKenzie's book, *The Spirit of St. Andrews.* "We have to think, to concentrate on the stroke in order to hit the ball correctly. In the same way, we want our golf courses to make us think. However much we enjoy whaling the life out of the little white ball, we soon grow tired of playing a golf course that does not give us problems in strategy as well as skill. All his courses that I have played have been interesting. In every instance, he has placed interest and enjoyment ahead of difficulty."

MacKenzie, who was born in England but died in Santa Cruz, California, not long after the inaugural Masters tournament in 1934, always credited Jones's input at Augusta National.

"An ideal golf course," Jones once said, "must give pleasure to everyone, including the veriest dub. There must always be an

Alister
MacKenzie

alternative route for everyone, and thought should be required as well as mechanical skill, and above all, it should never be hopeless for the duffer, nor fail to concern and interest the duffer."

MacKenzie's masterpiece is Cypress Point on northern California's scenic coast, a course that Frank ("Sandy") Tatum, a longtime USGA official, once described as the "Sistine Chapel of golf."

In a *Golf Digest* survey in 1982, some fifty pro and amateur golfers, officials, celebrities, and authors were asked, "If you only had one course to play for the rest of your life, which one would it be?" Cypress Point received the most votes: fifteen. Augusta National was a distant second, with four. Pebble Beach and Merion each got three.

But strangely, MacKenzie's design of Cypress Point does not conform to what many golf people consider the essence of a championship course, that it finish with three or four long holes.

Instead, it finishes with four relatively short holes, beginning with successive par-3 holes—the 139-yard 15th over rocks where surf crashes to a green tucked into a grassy plateau and the 233-yard 16th over the dazzlingly scenic ocean inlet to a plateau green—and concluding with two par 4s—the 375-yard sharp dogleg right 17th along the rocks and the 339-yard angled dogleg right 18th uphill through a narrow gap in the trees to the green.

"Two one-shot holes and two drive-and-pitch holes," MacKenzie once said, "and yet I think it is the most exact and terrifying finish of any course I know."

MacKenzie, who was born in England and designed courses there as well as in Scotland, Australia, and New Zealand, died in 1934 not far from Cypress Point, a few miles up the California coast in Santa Cruz, where he lived in a small home off the 6th hole at Pasatiempo, another course he had designed. But for all his success and popularity as a golf architect, he always insisted that St. Andrews was golf's best course.

"St. Andrews is first class," he said, "there is no second, and Cypress Point comes a very bad third."

One of MacKenzie's pet peeves was anyone who considered a "complete island short hole a good one." To him, "Holes of this type can never be considered completely satisfying, as only one shot is required, namely the monotonous pitch." That philosophy, of course, has been defied by Pete Dye, who created what is now golf's most famous, or infamous, island hole—the 132-yard 17th at the Tournament Players Club at Sawgrass in Ponte Vedra, Florida, the site of the annual Players Championship on the PGA Tour.

"I decided," Dye once said, "if I was ever going to be known, I had to do something different."

His 17th hole at the Tournament Players Club certainly was different, the essence of penal golf-course design. Since the first Players Championship there in 1982, thousands of golf balls have splashed into the lake, with its resident alligator, that virtually surrounds the green. Most of those balls belonged to visiting duffers, but more than a few belonged to the touring pros who missed the green in the Players Championship.

Dye, a former insurance salesman, is also known for using wooden railroad ties to shore up banks and bunkers, prompting the joke that he builds the only courses that could burn down.

Another joke in golf architecture was that Jack Nicklaus, early in his career, designed courses only he could play. For anyone else, they simply were too difficult, with too many long carries from the tee, with too many long irons to the greens, with too much undulation in the greens. But over the years, the Golden Bear learned to ease the demands of his courses, even his masterpiece, Muirfield Village near Columbus, Ohio. Over more than two decades, he has designed more than one hundred fifty courses in twenty-four countries.

The most expensive golf course is believed to be Shadow Creek in Las Vegas, Nevada, which Tom Fazio designed for Steve Wynn, the owner of the Mirage hotel-casino there, for some $40 million.

"I don't care what it costs," Wynn told Fazio when they inspected the three hundred fifty acres of desert scrub where the course was to be created. "Buy what you have to buy; get what you have to get."

Fazio's bulldozers dug sixty feet into the desert floor as his crew created a half-mile creek bed with ponds and waterfalls. He brought in ten thousand trees for $9 million and miles of sod for another $4 million.

For all the new architects, Robert Trent Jones's influence is still thriving in the sense that his sons, Rees and Bobby, are now two of the busiest course designers. Bobby has designed more than one hundred in thirty-three countries, and Rees, while also creating more than one hundred, is now considered the U.S. Open Doctor, since he has restyled several famous courses for the U.S. Open.

"My father," Rees Jones said, "was trying to thwart the efforts of the pros, make things tougher and tougher. We're trying to find the proper champion by penalizing the shot to the degree that it's been missed."

ARNOLD PALMER WAS PLAYING A PRACTICE ROUND before the 1989 British Open at Royal Troon when a photographer asked him to pose for a picture.

"I'd like you," the photographer said, "standing next to the plaque in the rough where you hit that famous shot."

Palmer smiled. He remembered the shot well, a slashing 6-iron out of thick high grass to within 15 feet of the flagstick on the 15th hole to win the 1961 British Open. Now he and the photographer started searching in the rough for the small plaque commemorating that shot. When they couldn't find it, Palmer turned to where his Scottish caddie, Tip Anderson, was still standing in the fairway.

"Where's the plaque?" Palmer asked.

"About four hundred miles away," the caddie said, rolling his eyes. "You're on the wrong course."

"Oh," Palmer said, laughing.

Now he remembered. He had hit that shot at Royal Birkdale in England to win the 1961 British Open, not at Troon on Scotland's western coast, where he won the 1962 British Open. But the enduring moral of that story is the importance of a good caddie to a touring pro or a duffer, whether suggesting the proper club or reading the line of a putt. Or recalling the correct site of a plaque commemorating a famous shot.

In big tournaments, caddies are part valet, part coach, part psychiatrist, and mostly invisible, but some have emerged as minicelebrities, known usually by their nicknames or first names.

Over the years, caddies have been known as Tip and Fluff and

Gypsy Joe and Iron Man and Cemetery and Squeeky and Golf Ball and Rabbit and sometimes by their real names, like Bruce and Angelo.

When Tiger Woods won the 1997 Masters, he credited Mike ("Fluff") Cowan for his knowledge of Augusta National's undulating greens after having been touring pro Peter Jacobsen's caddie there for nearly two decades.

"I think Fluff's the best caddie in the world," Woods said. "Our relationship is more like two great friends playing out there."

When Woods decided to try the PGA Tour after having won his third straight U.S. Amateur title in 1996, he needed a week-to-week pro caddie. At the time, Jacobsen was recuperating from a back ailment, so Fluff was available. In the hours when Woods was still celebrating his U.S. Amateur victory, Fluff got a phone call.

Tiger Woods trusts Fluff Cowan's opinion.

"I'm turning pro this week," Woods said. "I plan on playing the next seven events. How many of those can you work for me?"

All seven, of course. Even so, Fluff considered it just a temporary job until Jacobsen was ready to return. But after only 9 holes of their practice round before Woods's pro debut in the Milwaukee Open, Fluff knew this young Tiger was somebody special.

"I started seeing these outrageous golf shots," he recalls. "Everything he did was completely fearless."

By the start of their fourth week together, their partnership was permanent, with Fluff getting 10 percent of Tiger's tour earnings, the standard fee for a tour caddie. But now Fluff had to tell Jacobsen that after more than nineteen years together, he would be carrying somebody else's bag.

"I'm happy for Fluff," Jacobsen said after recovering from the shock. "It couldn't have happened to a better guy."

Not that Fluff thinks he's really responsible for all those 300-yard drives and dartlike irons that Woods hits.

"Any caddie who thinks he makes the player is wrong," Fluff has said. "It's the player who makes the caddie. We are not the show. Any caddie who thinks he's the show, he's not going to last long."

Jeff Medlen, known as Squeeky because of his high-pitched voice, had that same humility until he died in 1997 of leukemia.

"To see Squeeky go at forty-three, such a nice guy," said Ernie Els, the two-time U.S. Open champion. "It's unfair to see him go like that. He was such an honest, dear man, you couldn't help but like the guy. He was always trying to motivate you. He'd always say, 'Good shot.'"

Squeeky didn't even lug Els's bag. Squeeky worked for Nick Price, the two-time PGA champion and 1994 British Open champion, who cherished him. In a twist of fate, when Price withdrew from the 1991 PGA Championship at Crooked Stick near Indianapolis to be with his wife, Sue, at the birth of their son, Gregory, his replacement in the tournament was John Daly, the designated alternate. Daly hired Squeeky for the week, and together they won the title. But the next

Nick Price
shares the 1994
PGA trophy with
Squeeky Medlen.

year and again in 1994, Squeeky was at the side of the PGA champi-on, this time Nick Price.

"When I'm on the practice range, Squeeky is really my eyes," Price said at the time. "He personally checks my aim and alignment, and that keeps me on target."

But the morning of the second round of the 1996 Motorola Western Open, Price was on the practice range and Squeeky wasn't. He was on a pay phone with a doctor in Columbus, Ohio, who told him the dreaded word: *leukemia*. After he was hospitalized, other PGA Tour caddies wore small green ribbons, their way of letting him know they were praying for him. But within a year, he was dead.

"I miss him," Price said. "I will always miss him."

Good caddies create that bond with a golfer, whether it's a profes-sional caddie in tournaments on the PGA Tour or a teenage caddie on a weekend morning at a local course. Once upon a time, caddies were available at almost every course for those who didn't want to carry their golf bags. But some golfers soon preferred pull carts, also known as trolleys. And once golfers started riding electric or gas carts, the supply of caddies dwindled, to the detriment of the game, many think. Youngsters who are caddies are more likely to become golfers, especially at private clubs that allow them to play for free on Monday, when the course is normally closed.

Many golfers believe that they play better with a good caddie, especially on an unfamiliar course where a good caddie knows the hazardous areas to avoid as well as the subtle breaks on the greens.

Since even a good caddie is unlikely to know a golfer's distance with each club, many golfers prefer to be advised of the yardage to the pin or to the front of the green. Once they know the yardage, they'll choose the club that fits their game's yardage. But for a youngster eager to make money as a caddie, there are twelve basic rules:

> Know all fourteen clubs in the bag.
> Hand the player the club he or she selects.
> Stand still.
> Keep quiet.
> Watch the ball.
> Replace all divots.
> Smooth the sand in the bunkers.
> The first caddie on the green takes the flag.
> Keep up with the player.
> Never swing a club.
> Memorize the yardage on each hole.
> If you don't know, ask.

Those rules are the same now as they were when Francis Ouimet insisted on using little ten-year-old Eddie Lowery as his caddie in his historic 1913 U.S. Open playoff with Harry Vardon and Ted Ray. Ouimet had used his neighborhood friend during the four rounds at The Country Club near Boston, but on the way to the 1st tee of the playoff, one of Ouimet's best friends, Frank Hoyt, approached him.

"May I carry your clubs?" Hoyt asked.

"You must ask Eddie," Ouimet replied.

Hoyt made an offer, but Lowery refused it. Hoyt upped his offer, but when Lowery again refused, Hoyt appealed to Ouimet, who turned to the little boy standing with his clubs.

"I looked at little Eddie, his eyes filled," Ouimet later recalled. "I think he was fearful that I would turn him down. I did not have the heart to take the clubs away from him."

And that day, with little ten-year-old Eddie Lowery carrying his clubs, Ouimet won the U.S. Open.

Ouimet understood Lowery's feelings. He had been a caddie himself, as many of America's best golfers were in those years before and after World War I, notably Gene Sarazen, Byron Nelson, Ben Hogan, and Sam Snead. Nelson and Hogan even grew up together in the same caddie yard at the Glen Garden Country Club in Fort Worth, Texas. In the 1927 9-hole caddie championship there, Nelson sank a long putt on the last green to tie Hogan. Each shot 40, 3 over par. In their playoff, Nelson won by 1 stroke. His prize was a 5-iron, Hogan's a 2-iron.

Nick Faldo and Fanny Sunesson climb Augusta National.

"But I already had a five and Ben already had a two," Nelson recalled years later. "So we traded clubs."

Although most of the PGA Tour caddies are men, Fanny Sunesson proved with Nick Faldo that a woman can do the job.

Growing up in Karlshamn, a harbor town in southern Sweden, she participated in judo and curling as well as golf. With a 5 handicap, she played the Swedish amateur tour and, with her

mother, won the Swedish mother-and-daughter championship. But in 1986, she decided to be a caddie.

"I wanted inside the ropes," she says. "I wanted to learn some shots, see how really good golfers played this game."

She hung around a Stockholm tournament in 1986, hoping to get a job. Jaime Gonzalez of Brazil eventually hired her.

"Until Jaime," she says, "I tried to get hired by everyone and anyone, but they all thought I didn't know anything because I was a girl. Once they saw me work, though, they caught on that I did know what I was doing."

In 1987, she helped Jose Rivero of Spain win the French Open. In 1989, she helped Howard Clark, an Englishman, make the European Ryder Cup team. One night in Australia late that year, she got a phone call from Faldo.

"Would you like to work for me?" he asked.

They were an instant success together. As Faldo won both the Masters and the British Open in 1990, Fanny could be seen hurrying along behind him, carrying a golf bag with forty pounds of clubs, balls, rain gear, fruit, granola bars, and water.

"She's keen on working hard," Faldo said. "She makes very few mistakes, and this is what makes a good team."

But all the attention embarrassed her. She's reluctant to talk to reporters or to be interviewed on television.

"At first," she once explained, "being a caddie was more like an adventure for me. To travel, see new countries, meet new cultures. Now this is my job, and I take it very seriously. But I'm not the one hitting the ball. I don't want to be a famous person back home in Sweden. When I'm home, I just want to be Fanny Sunesson, not the girl who's carrying Nick Faldo's bag."

In Asia, caddies are often women or teenage girls, but the first female caddie at the Masters was George Archer's then sixteen-year-old daughter, Liz.

Archer, the 1969 Masters winner, had caddied while growing up in San Mateo, California, where he often watched Byron Nelson and Ken Venturi play. As somebody who admittedly doesn't "like a lot of conversation" when he's playing, he preferred a caddie who wouldn't talk too much during the 1980 Masters. But after he hit a bad drive, his daughter Liz spoke up.

"Dad," she said, "can I say something?"

"What's that?" her father wondered.

"I want to tell you that I love you."

At the Masters, the pros now use their regular tour caddies, but until 1982 they had to use the Augusta National caddies, some of whom were known mostly by their nicknames. Iron Man carried Arnold Palmer's bag. Cemetery read the greens for President Eisenhower whenever he visited. One story involved an apparently inexperienced caddie who was carrying Dutch Harrison's bag one day in the early years of the Masters. At the long uphill par-5 8th hole, Harrison hit a big drive. Arriving at his ball, he turned to his caddie.

"Can I get home from here?" Harrison asked.

"Mr. Dutch, I don't even know where you live."

George Archer and his daughter Liz at the 1980 Masters

But the most memorable golfer-and-caddie scene developed at the 1986 Masters when forty-six-year-old Jack Nicklaus shot a 30 on the back 9 for a 7-under-par 65 and won his sixth green jacket. He had trudged up the hill to the 18th green with his oldest son, Jackie, in white coveralls, carrying his bag. When he sank what would be the winning putt, he hugged his twenty-four-year-old son as the applause thundered.

"To have your son with you in that situation, it's a great experience for him and for me," he said later. "On the putts, Jackie kept telling me, 'You'll get this birdie. Just keep your head still.' I have a tendency to move my head when I putt, but he helped me keep it still. He's a good kid. I have great admiration for him. He's handled the burden of my name. I'm happy to have him part of this."

But Jack Nicklaus wasn't any happier than his caddie was.

ON THE TEE, THE SWING'S THE THING

TIGER WOODS SWUNG HIS DRIVER, AND HIS BALL SOARED high in the sky as Nick Price watched. From the tee on the 533-yard 7th hole at the Tournament Players Club at Las Colinas near Dallas, the ball would roll to a stop about 330 yards away in the fairway. Awed by the power and accuracy of that tee shot, a young man in the gallery yelled, "I did that in my dreams last night."

"So did I," Price said, smiling.

Tiger Woods's drives are the envy of PGA Tour pros, not merely for their length but, more importantly, because his golf ball is usually in the fairway. In driving contests, some long hitters have smashed tee shots more than 400 yards, but when those long hitters are actually playing golf, their tee shots sometimes wind up in the trees, on another fairway, or out of bounds.

Hitting a long tee shot doesn't mean much if you can't find your ball, or if, when you do find it, you either can't hit it or it's out of bounds in somebody's backyard.

Woods learned that lesson the hard way. Whenever he was out of contention in tournaments, it usually was because his tee shots strayed into high rough or the trees.

In developing what Ben Hogan once described as a "correct, powerful, repeating swing," accuracy is the most important factor, whether you're hitting a driver or any other club off the tee. On the PGA Tour or the LPGA Tour, the winner of the weekly tournament isn't always the golfer who hits the longest tee shots, it's the golfer who shoots the lowest score. And that golfer invariably is the one whose golf swing was the most dependable under pressure that week.

For every golfer, pro or duffer, the search for a better golf swing never ends, because the search for a better score never ends.

The golf swing is so elusive, so dependent on even the slightest variation in where the club head strikes the ball, that it changes almost day to day. When Al Geiberger was the first player on the PGA Tour to break 60, shooting a 13-under-par 59 at the 1977 Memphis (Tennessee) Classic, his swing and his putting stroke were so dependable, he made 11 birdies and 1 eagle (when he holed an 80-yard wedge shot). But he never came close to shooting 59 again, proof that in a golf swing, every day is a new day, for better or for worse.

For any golfer, the best way to develop a golf swing is to take lessons from the teaching pro at your favorite course or driving range.

During those lessons, you'll learn the proper grip, the proper stance and posture, the proper backswing, the proper downswing, and the proper follow-through. If you don't take lessons, you'll be making mistakes. You'll develop bad habits that will be hard to break and might haunt you all your life.

If you can't afford to take lessons, try to copy the swings of the best golfers on television, study their instruction videos, or read their instruction books.

But more than anything else, be willing to practice. The pros hit hundreds of golf balls almost every day on the range, some as many as a thousand balls. In his devotion to golf, Ben Hogan remembered hitting "thousands and thousands of balls to find out exactly what happens in the swing; then I took that and determined what would work out on the course under pressure." For all their practice, no two golfers swing exactly the same way, but their fundamentals of grip, stance, and posture will be similar and, no matter what the difference in their backswing, their club face will be square to the ball at impact.

Good swings endure, as proved by the two golfers whom most

historians consider to have had the sweetest swings—Sam Snead and Mickey Wright.

On his eighty-fifth birthday in 1997, Snead shot 78 at the Greenbrier resort in White Sulphur Springs, West Virginia, with basically the same swing that he had sixty years earlier when he and his friend, Johnny Bulla, joined the PGA Tour.

"I've seen 'em all from Walter Hagen to now," Bulla said that day at the Greenbrier, "and no-body ever swung a club with the rhythm that Sam has."

Snead's swing endured as few have. When he was sixty-eight years old, he shot 68–67 to win the 1980 *Golf Digest* Commemorative Pro-Am at the Newport (Rhode Island) Country Club and impressed Bob Toski, a renowned professor of the golf swing who was once a leading PGA Tour player.

"Sam still has that loping, silken motion," Toski said, "that for generations has made his swing the standard by which all others are measured."

At the Greenbrier resort, which Snead represented for much of

**Sam Snead's
sweetest swing**

his career, they tell the story about the big tree out about 200 yards on the practice range. When he was practicing there with a 2-iron, he would hit ten balls over the top of the tree, draw ten balls from right-to-left around the tree, and fade ten balls from left-to-right around the tree.

"After those thirty shots," said Bill Campbell, the West Virginia amateur, "you could go out there and throw a blanket over the thirty balls."

That's what pros call "being able to shape" a shot, hitting it high or low with a draw or a fade. Throughout Snead's career, other pros would stop to watch him on the practice range. One day, he hit a towering tee shot and said, "I'd like a million of those." Hearing that, another pro, Dave Hill, said, "Sam, you've already had a million of those."

Mickey Wright's swing prompted the same adulation when she appeared, at age fifty-eight, at the 1993 Sprint Senior Challenge in Tallahassee, Florida.

Kris Tschetter, an LPGA pro who had developed a friendship with Ben Hogan, described Wright as "our legend, and she still swings every bit like a legend." By then, Wright had been off the LPGA Tour for more than a quarter of a century, but her swing was the same.

"To me," Wright once said, "golf means one thing and always will—the pure pleasure I get from swinging a golf club."

Among today's golfers, one of the smoothest swings belongs to Ernie Els, the big South African who won the U.S. Open in 1994 at Oakmont and again at Congressional in 1997. That swing was never smoother under pressure than it was on the last 2 holes at Congressional against Tom Lehman, Jeff Maggert, and England's Colin Montgomerie.

Needing 2 pars to win, Els hit a perfect drive on the downhill dogleg 480-yard 17th, then "the best 5-iron of my life" from 212 yards to 17 feet beyond the hole on the green that juts out into a lake. He

2-putted for par. On the 190-yard 18th, he floated a 7-iron over the water into the middle of the green, about 20 feet away. He 2-putted to win another U.S. Open.

Even before that second U.S. Open victory, Els's swing had already entranced his guru, David Leadbetter.

"His rhythm is superb," Leadbetter once said of his 6–4, 210-pound student. "That's what he's always trying to work on—trying to stay soft, not have any hurry in his swing. What he likes to do is swing soft; his smoothness is really a joy to behold. Getting into the impact area, you can see how well his head stays behind the ball. At the release, his head is still well behind, and there is beautiful extension through the shot. You can see where he unleashes all the power. He finishes in a beautifully balanced position, a classic finish where his right shoulder is all the way through to the target."

Els started playing at age seven with his father, the way many touring pros begin, but not all. Seve Ballesteros, the Spanish golf genius, also started playing at age seven, but with a 3-iron head fitted to a stick for a shaft.

"I used pebbles for golf balls," Ballesteros recalled. "The next year, my brother Manuel, the second oldest of my three brothers, gave me a real 3-iron and some real golf balls. Caddies at my home course in Pedreña were allowed few liberties when I was a boy, so I had to practice on the beach, or in the fields behind my family's farmhouse. On the beach, I would design two or three holes on the hard, wet sand that had been smoothed by the sea. Practicing on the beach turned out to be an invaluable experience. Striking the ball cleanly from the sand helps to teach you great touch and club-head control."

Tiger Woods developed touch and club-head control at an even earlier age, but what makes his golf swing special is its combination of power and accuracy.

"You couldn't teach Tiger's swing, and there's nothing wrong with it," the legendary Byron Nelson said shortly after Woods won the

1997 Masters. "His balance is great. He never moves off the ball. His timing, his movement, his coordination are excellent. His swing is just one continuous motion. He's got a great feel for how hard to hit the ball. His swing is a motion here," meaning the backswing, "and a motion there, fast and hard," meaning his downswing and follow-through. "And his club-head speed is so fast, you don't even see his hands."

Woods's club-head speed has reportedly been clocked at a remarkable 178 miles per hour, but his "feel for how hard to hit the ball," according to Nelson, "is why he can pitch the ball to the green so well with his wedge," whether it's from 100 yards, 120 yards, or 150 yards.

But on the golf course, your golf swing is only as good as both your muscle memory in repeating that swing and your mental approach to making the shot. If you don't think you can carry that pond in front of the tee or that bunker in front of the green, you probably won't. Negative thoughts breed negative shots, just as positive thoughts breed positive shots, especially with the longer clubs. In needing a par 4 on the final hole of the final round in the 1995 U.S. Open at Shinnecock Hills, Corey Pavin proved the importance of positive thoughts.

On the tee, as Pavin recalled later, he "had to hit the ball in the fairway" and he did. Now he had 228 yards to the hole and chose his 4-wood.

"I then started planning how to play the shot," he said later, "speaking my thoughts aloud to affirm to myself that I was thinking clearly: 'I'll aim at the right edge of the green with a little draw and let the wind carry the ball toward the hole.' By aiming to the right, I took the trouble to the left of the green out of play."

Pavin swung his 4-wood, his ball took off low and began to draw to the left on a line to the hole. It landed short of the green, bounced up, and rolled toward the hole.

"I thought for a minute it might roll into the hole," he recalled.

"From my vantage point, all I could see was the ball and the flagstick. I couldn't wait. I started running toward the hole. When I saw the ball was within five feet of the pin, I managed to slow down to a walk."

Corey Pavin missed his 5-foot putt, then carefully made the 1-foot putt that would win the U.S. Open, but his solid swing in hitting that 4-wood from 228 yards had really won it.

IT HAD A 6-IRON CLUB HEAD ATTACHED TO ONE END, BUT it wasn't really a golf club. It was an instrument that Alan Shepard had used to collect rock and dust samples on the moon. But now, on February 6, 1971, as dawn broke over the Atlantic coast of the United States and just before the *Apollo 14* spacecraft would leave the moon for its return to earth, the forty-seven-year-old astronaut in the bulky space suit dropped two golf balls onto the whitish gray soil and hit them.

"I shanked the first one; it rolled into a crater about forty yards away," he told *Golf Journal*, the official USGA magazine, twenty-five years later. "The second one, I kept my head down. I hit it flush and it went at least two hundred yards."

Alan Shepard hit golf's two most celebrated iron shots about two hundred fifty thousand miles away from the nearest course, but with no vegetation, no wind, no rain, and no sound, how did he know that his second shot floated at least two hundred yards?

"The reason I know," he said, "is that I planned to hit it down-sun, against a black sky so I could follow the trajectory of the ball. That happened to be the direction we had paced off two hundred meters for our experimental field, and it landed just past that area. I folded up the club, put it in my pocket, climbed up the ladder, closed the door, and we took off."

At the time, of course, Shepard joked that he had hit that second ball several miles, what he called a "slight exaggeration" that no golfer could resist. But the shots had a scientific purpose.

"All of us who were lucky to be on the surface of the moon," he

Alan Shepard walks on the moon.

explained, "tried to think of something that would demonstrate the lack of gravity, the lack of atmosphere. The classic example of dropping a feather and a lead ball had already been done. But then I thought that with the same club-head speed, the ball is going to go six times as far. There's absolutely no drag, so if you do happen to spin it, it won't slice or hook because there's no atmosphere to make it turn."

In the weeks before the *Apollo 14* soared into space from Cape Kennedy, Florida, on January 31, 1971, Shepard had taken the space instrument to Jack Harden, the golf pro at the River Oaks Country Club in Houston, Texas, near the Johnson Space Center. Harden quickly attached a 6-iron club head. But on the moon, Shepard's space suit restricted his swing.

"The suit was so clumsy, being pressurized, it was impossible to get two hands comfortably on the handle, and it was impossible to make any kind of turn," Shepard said. "My swing was kind of a one-handed chili-dip. As for what brand the golf balls were, I wanted it to be without any commercial aspects. Only one person knows the trade name of the golf balls. That's me."

Whatever brand they were, those two golf balls probably don't exist anymore.

"They've probably melted in the heat," Shepard said, "or exploded in the cold."

Weather conditions aren't that severe on earth. Golfers don't need to wear bulky space suits to hit their irons, the clubs designed for accuracy to the green or for getting the ball out of the rough. When a young touring pro once mentioned to Ben Hogan that he was having trouble with his long putts, the four-time U.S. Open champion stared at him.

"Why," Hogan suggested, "don't you try hitting your irons closer to the pin?"

Hogan wasn't joking. He spent hours practicing with all his clubs, especially all his irons. Because the 1-iron has the least loft of any of the irons, it's the most difficult to hit consistently well. Lee Trevino jokes that in a lightning storm, a golfer should hold his 1-iron aloft "because only God can hit a one-iron," meaning hit it with a lightning bolt.

Trevino indeed was joking because, more than most golfers, he knows to get off the course when lightning is flashing. During a rain delay in the 1975 Western Open, he was struck by lightning while sitting near a green close to a pond.

Jokes aside, Hogan hit arguably the most crucial 1-iron in history. In the final round of the 1950 U.S. Open at Merion outside Philadelphia, he needed a par 4 on the final hole to force a playoff. After a good drive, he was about 200 yards from what he described as an "elusive, well-trapped, slightly plateaued green." Not a routine shot, especially with a 1-iron. But he remembered how "the ball took off on a line for the left-center of the green, held its line firmly, bounced on the front edge of the green, and finished some forty feet from the cup. It was all I could have asked for." He 2-putted to create the 18-hole playoff he would win from Lloyd Mangrum and George Fazio.

That 1-iron is remembered as the shot that certified Hogan's comeback from the head-on collision of his car with a bus sixteen months earlier, but he remembered it differently.

"I didn't hit that shot then, that late afternoon at Merion," he wrote in *Five Lessons: The Modern Fundamentals of Golf.* "I'd been practicing that shot since I was twelve years old. After all, the point of tournament golf is to get command of a swing which, the more pressure you put on it, the better it works."

In the 1974 U.S. Open, Hale Irwin hit a similar shot with a 2-iron. Going to the final hole of the final round, Irwin had a 2-shot lead. With a par 4, he would win by 2. With a bogey, he would win by 1. But on the 448-yard 18th hole at Winged Foot, a dogleg left to an undulating green, a double-bogey is always lurking.

Irwin hit an accurate drive into the middle of the fairway, then drilled a 2-iron into the heart of the 18th green, about 20 feet from the cup.

"I hadn't hit the two-iron well in the first two rounds, but I still had confidence in it," Irwin said. "At that stage, it was the shot of my life."

Irwin had practiced hitting his 2-iron, just as Hogan had practiced hitting his 1-iron and as Nick Faldo had practiced hitting his 3-iron long before the 1992 British Open at Muirfield, when he chose that club for his shot to the final green in the final round. Two strokes behind John Cook as he left the 14th green that day, Faldo told himself, "Somehow you'd better play the best four holes of your life." He did.

After birdies at the 15th and the 17th, Faldo needed to par the

18th to win. After a big drive, he had 197 yards to the pin from virtually the same spot where Cook had pushed a 2-iron en route to a bogey. With his 3-iron, Faldo faded his ball slightly to hold it steady against a strong right-to-left crosswind. It nearly hit the pin and rolled to about 20 feet away. Two putts and he had won his third British Open.

"I thought I had blown it," Faldo said later, close to tears. "It's the enormity of it all. The pressure is so great, but I turned it around. I went from the brink of disaster to the absolute ultimate."

With that 3-iron, Faldo won despite the wind that often affects the flight of the ball, for better or for worse. With the wind at your back, the ball will soar farther than usual. With the wind coming from the right or the left, the ball will be blown that way. With the wind against you, the ball won't go as far as you usually hit it. Especially the wind that often howls across a British Open links course, as Tiger Woods discovered in 1997 at Royal Troon when he hit a 4-iron.

"It just ballooned up in the air," he said with a sorry smile. "It only went one hundred forty-five yards."

Woods usually hits a 4-iron at least 225 yards—that's how hard the wind was blowing that day at Royal Troon on Scotland's western coast. But when there is no wind, a touring pro is usually able to hit the ball to a virtually precise distance with each of his irons. One of those precise shots developed on the final hole of the 1976 U.S. Open at the Atlanta Athletic Club after Jerry Pate surveyed his approach from 190 yards in the rough over a pond to the flagstick.

"Even though I had a great lie, I was convinced it was a four-iron," Pate has often said, "but my caddie, John Considine, kept telling me it was a five-iron."

Whichever iron Pate was considering, Tom Weiskopf and Al Geiberger were already in at 279. To win, Pate needed a par 4 on the 460-yard 18th hole. He decided to take his caddie's advice. He swung his 5-iron; the ball soared high above the pond and dove at the flagstick, stopping 3 feet away. He made the birdie putt for 277, a winner by 2 strokes.

"If I'd hit the four-iron like I wanted to, who knows what would've happened," Pate said. "That's why a good caddie means so much."

Just as astronaut Alan Shepard hit a 6-iron off the moon's whitish gray soil, golfers sometimes must hit their irons off the sand in fairway bunkers. Which iron they use depends on how far they are from the green, but one of golf's most memorable 7-iron shots occurred in the 1988 Masters after Sandy Lyle's tee shot on the final hole settled into the sand of the long bunker on the left side of the fairway.

Lyle, a thirty-year-old Scot, needed a par to tie Mark Calcavecchia and create a sudden-death playoff, but with his tee shot in that bunker, a par would not be easy. As for a winning birdie, not since

Sandy Lyle's bunker shots made the difference in the 1988 Masters.

LEADERS

	HOLE	1	2	3	4	5	6	7	8	9	10	11	12	13	14	15	16	17	18
PRIOR	PAR	4	5	4	3	4	3	4	5	4	4	4	3	5	4	5	3	4	4
6	LYLE	6	7	7	8	8	7												
4	CRENSHAW	3	4	5	5	5	4												
4	CALCAVECCHIA	4	5	5	4	4	3	2											
2	LANGER	2	3	3	2	2	2	■											
2	COUPLES	2	3	3	2	2	2	2											
2	ZOELLER	3	3	2	2	2	1	1											
1	POOLEY	2	3	4	3	3	2	2	3	3									

THRU 6

MESSAGE FOR

Arnold Palmer in 1960 had a golfer come to the 18th green at Augusta National, knowing he needed a birdie to win and then making that birdie to win. But out of a bunker 143 yards away? Hardly. If anything, a losing bogey was more likely.

"I personally thought it was over," Lyle said later. "That front bunker has a very steep face. I didn't think I'd have a chance of getting to the green. But it was up the face and I had a good lie."

Thanks to a good swing, Lyle's ball soared out of the sand, toward the green, and at the flagstick. Landing high on the green with backspin, it stopped, then rolled slowly down the hill toward the cup, to within 20 feet, then 15 feet, then 10 feet. Lyle now could win by making that putt. And he did.

"My knees were knocking a bit," he said later, "but that was the straightest putt I had all week."

Golfers have made a hole in one with every club, from driver to sand-wedge, but Tom Watson made a hole in one with an 8-iron at the 1980 U.S. Open after suggesting to USGA officials that they not use the pin position near the front of the 4th green at Baltusrol because the grass was pockmarked.

"But when I got to the fourth tee in the first round," Watson has recalled, "that's where the pin was—down in that pockmarked area."

That pockmarked area is where Watson's ball landed before disappearing into the cup, to the roar of the gallery around the green. But one of the loudest roars in golf history accompanied the disappearance of a golf ball into the cup on the 162-yard 16th hole in the 1997 Phoenix Open at the Tournament Players Club at Scottsdale, Arizona. As soon as that roar resounded, Nick Price knew what had happened, even though he was near the clubhouse.

"Had to be an ace," he said. "Had to be Tiger."

It was an ace and it was Tiger Woods, who had used a 9-iron. It was his 9th ace, his 2nd as a pro after only ten pro tournaments. But unlike astronaut Alan Shepard, he's never hit a golf ball on the moon. Yet.

AS THE 1997 BRITISH OPEN CHAMPION, JUSTIN LEONARD suddenly was one of golf's new faces. But a few weeks later, the night before the 1997 PGA Championship began at Winged Foot, the twenty-five-year-old Texan attended a reception honoring one of golf's legends, Byron Nelson, the eighty-five-year-old Texan.

"He sat me down," Leonard recalled after a 2-under-par 68 the next day, "and told me, 'On this course, you're going to make bogeys and so is everybody else. When you hit it in the rough, just get it down there to where you've got an eight-iron or a nine-iron or a wedge or a sand-wedge in your hands. You'll get a few up and down.'"

Justin Leonard, a young master of the wedge

Leonard turned Nelson's advice into a display of wizardry with the wedge, the essence of what is known in golf as the short game.

From 60 yards on Winged Foot's 4th hole, he wedged to 3 feet. From 103 yards on the 11th hole, he wedged to 3 feet. From 79 yards on the 15th hole, he wedged to 4 feet. From 48 yards on the 16th hole, he wedged to 4 feet. And from 81 yards on the 17th hole, he wedged to 5 feet.

By getting up and down, as the pros say, with all those wedge shots and all those putts, Leonard shot 68 instead of at least 73.

"I had hoped that I wouldn't have to remember Byron Nelson's words as often as I did," he said, "but I think it was very special for him to pull me aside and give me advice."

It also was very wise for Leonard not only to accept Nelson's advice but also to follow it so successfully.

That's the value of a good short game—the wedge shots from around 100 yards or less, the sand-wedge shots from a greenside bunker, the chip shots from near the green. Those are the shots that enable a golfer to hit the ball close enough to get it in the hole with a short putt, thereby saving at least 1 stroke, if not 2 or 3.

The sand-wedge, now used as much off the fairway and out of the rough as it is in a bunker, was invented by Gene Sarazen in 1931. With a thicker sole, or flange, at the bottom than other clubs, it gets under the ball easier, especially in the sand or in heavy rough.

Until the sand-wedge, golfers had dreaded sand bunkers, especially those on the British seaside links. At the short 11th hole at St. Andrews during a British Amateur match, one golfer hit his ball into the Strath bunker while the other hit his ball into the Hill bunker. Each blasted out over the green, then kept spraying his golf ball in all directions. After 14 strokes each, their balls were exactly as they started, except their positions were reversed; the one who had hit into the Strath bunker originally was now in the Hill bunker, and vice versa. They finally halved, or tied, the hole with 17s.

Pros developed so much expertise with the sand-wedge that

some, notably Gary Player, preferred to put their ball into a greenside bunker rather than risk going into the nearby rough.

"Once you learn to hit a sand-wedge properly out of the sand," Player explained, "that is a much easier shot than trying to get the ball close to the pin from out of tangled grass."

In the 1988 U.S. Open at The Country Club outside Boston, Curtis Strange showed that expertise out of a bunker. Tied coming down the 438-yard 18th hole in the final round, Strange plunked his approach into a bunker in front of the green while Nick Faldo was on the green's fringe, about 40 feet away. To have any chance of forcing an 18-hole playoff, Strange needed to get down in 2.

"I just told myself, 'Do it,'" Strange would say later. "I reminded myself how many times I had this shot before, and all the times I hit a good shot. And when I saw the ball stop a foot away from the cup, I felt I could make that putt."

Curtis Strange blasting out during the 1988 U.S. Open at The Country Club

He did, for a par 4 while Faldo 2-putted for his par. In the playoff, Strange won, 71 to 75, and he would win the U.S. Open again in 1989 at Oak Hill, the first to do so in consecutive years since Ben Hogan won in 1950 and 1951. But if he had not gotten up and down from that bunker at The Country Club, he never would have won that first U.S. Open.

The wedge, in one form or another, had been around for nearly a century before it emerged in 1953 as a celebrity in golf's first nationally televised tournament, the Tam O'Shanter World Championship of Golf outside Chicago.

The tournament promoter, George S. May, had put up a first prize of twenty-five thousand dollars, a bonanza in a time when the U.S. Open and PGA champions each collected five thousand dollars, the Masters winner four thousand. All that prize money prompted the ABC television network to put a camera behind the 18th green for its one-hour show.

Chandler Harper, the 1950 PGA champion, finished at 279, the apparent winner until Lew Worsham, the 1947 U.S. Open champion, birdied the 17th hole. Worsham now could tie Harper with another birdie.

After a good drive on the final hole, Worsham had 104 yards to the flagstick. He chose what was known in those years as the MacGregor double-duty wedge because, as Worsham said, "you could use it off the fairway or out of the sand." But he had to hit his ball over a stream and between two trees.

"I was just hoping to get the ball on the green close enough for a birdie putt to tie for the lead," he once said. "After I hit it, it ran twenty-five or thirty feet. I thought it would be close, and the next thing I knew, it was in."

With that wedge shot for an eagle 2, not only had Worsham won the World Championship with its twenty-five-thousand-dollar jackpot and thirty-seven-thousand-dollar guarantee for exhibition

Lew Worsham's wedge shot: the swing, the bounce, the disappearance

matches, but he had also done it on national television for about a million viewers.

Holing a shot, as distinguished from a putt, to win on the final hole with that shot, is a rarity in golf. Dick Mayer, the 1957 U.S. Open champion, holed a 35-yard wedge to win the 1965 New Orleans Open. And it had never happened in a major tournament until the 1986 PGA Championship at Inverness when Bob Tway holed a 25-foot bunker shot from in front of the final green for a birdie 3 that snatched the title from Greg Norman.

"I was just trying to get it close enough for one putt," Tway said. "To make a shot like that, the odds against it, I don't even know. I may never make one of them again in my career."

When Tway's ball disappeared into the cup on the 354-yard finishing hole, Norman stood nearby in shock. He was on the front fringe of the green in 2, but now the Great White Shark needed to sink a 25-foot putt to tie. He missed, his ball rolling 10 feet past the cup. Tway had won.

Larry Mize whoops after his chip shot has disappeared into the cup to win the 1987 Masters.

The next year, on the 2nd hole of their sudden-death playoff in the 1987 Masters, Norman was victimized by another hole-out, this time by Larry Mize's chip shot with a sand-wedge.

Norman was on the edge of the green in 2, but Mize's 5-iron approach to the 455-yard 11th hole had faded to the right, stopping about 140 feet from the hole. But when Mize arrived at his ball, he noticed that his line to the pin was roughly the same as it had been earlier that day when he missed a 20-foot birdie putt.

"The greens were hard," he said later, "so I knew I had to bump it through the fringe. I hit it low so it wouldn't catch up. It just rolled up and went in."

Only eight months after watching Tway's shot disappear

into the cup on the 18th hole at the PGA, Norman again was in shock as Mize's ball disappeared into the cup on Augusta National's 2nd playoff hole.

"I didn't think Larry could get down in two," Norman said later. "And I was right. He got down in one."

On the LPGA Tour, Sally Little holed a 75-foot bunker shot at the 18th to win the 1976 Ladies International at Moss Creek in Hilton Head, South Carolina, by one stroke from Jan Stephenson. In the 1983 Hawaiian Open, Isao Aoki holed a 128-yard wedge shot for an eagle 3 that stunned Jack Renner.

Sally Little explodes her ball, and then her emotions explode as she wins the 1976 Ladies International.

"One hop, down," Aoki said later.

Doug Ford completed his 1957 Masters victory by holing a sand-wedge out of a bunker near the 18th green, but he finished 3 shots ahead. Arnold Palmer holed a delicate downhill chip with a wedge from 10 feet behind the 16th green in the final round of his 1960 Masters victory. In the final round of the 1972 British Open at Muirfield, Lee Trevino holed a 7-iron from off the 17th green to save a par 5, the difference in his 1-stroke triumph. The day before Trevino holed a sand-wedge from a treacherous downhill lie in the back of a bunker off the 16th green for a birdie 2.

"On that one," Trevino said, "the ball went in on the first bounce. If it hadn't, it might've rolled twenty feet past the hole."

But it didn't. His ball hit the flagstick and disappeared into the cup. That's what a good short game does. It wins tournaments.

PUTTING APPEARS TO BE THE EASIEST PART OF GOLF, BUT it's often the hardest. When the ball disappears into the cup that is 4.25 inches wide, it seems so simple. But when it doesn't disappear, when it spins off the lip, or when it stops near the cup, or when it stops nowhere near the cup, it's the most frustrating part of golf.

Considering that par on any hole includes 2 strokes for putting, it's also the most important part of golf. That 6-inch tap-in after a missed putt counts for 1 stroke just as much as a tee shot of 250 yards.

In match play, a putt is sometimes conceded or considered a "gimme" when the ball stops relatively close to the cup. But in stroke-play tournaments, whether in the U.S. Open or the British Open, whether on the PGA Tour or the LPGA Tour, there are no gimmes. Your ball must be putted out—even when a golfer's ball is only 1 inch from the hole, as Mark McCumber remembers only too well.

Mark McCumber is smiling here, but he didn't smile when he once missed a 1-inch putt.

As the defending champion in the 1988 Players Championship at the Tournament Players Club at Sawgrass in Ponte Vedra, Florida, McCumber hit a 9-iron to within 25 feet of the cup on the 132-yard 17th hole, the infamous "island hole." His 1st putt rolled about 4 feet past the cup. His 2nd putt spun off the lip to about 1 inch behind the cup.

As millions of other golfers have done in this situation, McCumber reached over with his putter to tap the ball in and take the ball out of the cup, all in the same motion. But the ball wasn't in the cup. In his haste, McCumber somehow had moved it only slightly, maybe a quarter of an inch. But that counted as a stroke.

Realizing he now had taken 3 putts, McCumber carefully tapped his ball into the cup with what amounted to his 4th putt for a double-bogey. Turning to Paul Azinger, who was playing with him, McCumber said, "I had five." Azinger, who apparently hadn't noticed the tap-in that hardly moved, looked over in disbelief.

"I hit it four times and it didn't go in," McCumber explained, "so I had to hit it again."

That's the essence of golf: hitting the ball until it's in the cup. Once you're on the green, the fewer putts the better. One of golf's oldest sayings is, "You drive for show, but you putt for dough." In the big tournaments, the winner is usually the golfer who makes the big putts, just as the loser is usually the golfer who misses the big putts.

The best golfers would not have been the best if they weren't among the best putters—Jack Nicklaus, Ben Hogan, Bobby Jones, Arnold Palmer, Tom Watson, Bobby Locke, Billy Casper, Kathy Whitworth, Nancy Lopez.

The putting style of each great putter has been as different as their actual putter—a blade, a mallet head, whatever it might be. In putting, you must be comfortable and confident in your stance and your stroke. But other factors exist. Your reading of the green, meaning if it's a straight putt or which way and how much your putt will break to the left or the right on its path to the hole. Your rhythm in

Billy Casper

setting the alignment of your putter blade. Your touch or your feel in stroking the putt in relation to the distance and the slope of the green. No matter what their stance and setup, the best putters all have that touch and feel.

"A man who can putt is a match for anyone," Willie Park, a four-time British Open champion, once said. "A man who can't putt is a match for no one."

As important as Jack Nicklaus's long drives and accurate irons were to his winning eighteen major titles as a pro, his putting often was the difference between winning and losing. In the final round of the 1986 Masters, his putts created birdies at the 9th, 10th, 11th, and 13th holes. On the 15th hole, he rolled into another putt for an eagle. At the 16th, another putt dropped for another birdie. Now, on the 17th green, he had an 11-footer for another birdie and the lead.

"I thought if I could make that one, I could win," he said later. "I did, and I did."

In the 1975 Masters, the Golden Bear was in a three-way duel with Tom Weiskopf and Johnny Miller as he surveyed a 40-foot putt on the 16th green. When it curled into the cup, he raised his putter high and danced off the green on the way to another green jacket.

"I was on the sixteenth tee watching," Weiskopf said later. "When that putt went in, I could see the Bear tracks on the green."

In his prime, Arnold Palmer seemed able almost to will the ball into the hole when he needed a putt. The higher the stakes, the better Palmer, like Nicklaus, was with a putter in his hands. But week in and week out, Billy Casper remains one of history's best putters. In winning the 1959 U.S. Open at Winged Foot, he needed only 114 putts over 72 holes, a remarkable average of only 28.5 putts a round on some of golf's fastest and most undulating greens.

In that same Open, Casper's confidence in his putting was obvious at the 209-yard 3rd hole. Instead of risking a tee shot into the deep bunkers on each side of the green that probably would result in a costly bogey, he laid up in front of the green in each round, chipped close to the hole, and 1-putted for his par.

"Billy had the greatest pair of hands that God ever gave a human being," Johnny Miller, the television analyst who won the 1973 U.S. Open, has said. "When you shook hands with Billy, he'd just give you the tips of his fingers, like a dead fish. He believed that his hands were so finely tuned that doing anything with force might mess up his touch."

Few golfers have had Ben Crenshaw's touch with a putter. As a teenager growing up in Austin, Texas, he learned to putt on the Bermuda-grass greens there.

"But when I went to the 1968 U.S. Junior Amateur at The Country Club outside Boston, that was the first time I ever putted on bent-grass greens," he once said. "I said to myself, 'This is easy. All you have to do is get the ball on line and it'll go in.'"

To him, all greens seem to be relatively easy. In winning the 1984 Masters, he holed a 60-foot birdie putt on the 10th green.

"It was probably the best putt I've ever hit," he once said. "I was just trying to leave myself within a radius of a couple feet from the hole, but when it was six feet away, I just knew it was going in. It was undoubtedly the key moment in the round. It was when I said to myself, 'Hey, this could be your week.'"

In some of golf's most dramatic scenarios, putting usually made the difference. Two of Tom Watson's five British Open triumphs turned on 2 long putts.

In 1977's final round, Watson was trailing Nicklaus by one shot at Turnberry as they walked to their tee shots on the 209-yard 15th hole. Nicklaus was on the green. Watson's ball had skidded a few feet off the green, about 60 feet from the hole. But a putter is often the best club to use from just off the green.

"I briefly thought about chipping," Watson recalled, "but I really had to go with the putter. I wasn't thinking of holing it, just getting it close. When I hit it, I knew the ball was moving a little bit too fast, but I also knew it was on line. Fortunately for me, the flagstick got in the way. That putt changed the tournament right there."

In the 1975 British Open, Watson knew he needed to sink a 25-foot birdie putt on the 18th hole of the final round.

"I had missed a lot of putts coming in, including a five-footer on the seventeenth," Watson said. "I knew I needed this twenty-five-footer to have a chance. When I made it, I almost strained my arm pumping the air."

In a playoff the next day, Watson defeated Jack Newton, 71 to 72, for his first of five British Open triumphs.

At his best, Watson was one of golf's most aggressive putters. When he missed, his ball often slid 3 or 4 feet past the cup, a dangerous distance. But he invariably made the comeback putt. However, in his later years, he fell into a putting slump. He kept missing putts from 3 or 4 feet, putts he never missed in his prime. In his frustration, only a few days before the 1996 Memorial at Muirfield Village, he was on the practice green at the Kansas City Country Club with Stan Thirsk, his teaching pro since he was six years old.

"You're hitting the putts solidly," Thirsk said.

"It doesn't feel that way," Watson said. "It feels like I'm hitting them on the toe of the putter instead of on the sweet spot in the middle."

"I'll prove you're hitting them in the middle," Thirsk said. "Don't go away."

Thirsk hurried into the nearby men's locker room and returned with a can of talcum powder. One by one, he patted a dab of the powder onto the golf balls that Watson had been putting, then set them down on the green with the powder in the area where it would be hit by Watson's putter.

"Now putt 'em," Thirsk said.

One by one, Watson putted, then looked down at the face of his putter. Each time he saw a dab of talcum powder in the middle of the sweet spot.

"Now do you believe me?" Thirsk asked. "Quit thinking about your mechanics and just go play."

The next week, Watson won the Memorial, his first victory on the PGA Tour in nine years. But his putting problems soon returned, as often happens with older golfers. They suffer from what golfers call the "yips," what Sam Snead once described as a lack of coordination stemming from the nerves that control the small muscles of the hand and wrist.

"If I only could putt," Snead often moaned.

For all the putts Snead missed, he made many more. If he hadn't, he wouldn't hold the PGA Tour record for tournament victories, with eighty-one. But to combat the yips in his later years, he went to a side-saddle style and then to the long putter.

"When you come in," Snead said, "they don't ask you how you did it; they just ask you what you shot."

Another putting method has evolved, called the cross-handed grip. Most right-handed golfers place their right hand below their left on their putter's handle. In the cross-handed grip, a right-handed golfer's left hand goes below the right.

"I have more stability," Nick Faldo said. "I just feel better putting this way."

The key word there is "feel," as in feeling the distance after reading the green and seeing the line, whatever the grip. And no matter how good a putter you might be, you're always going to miss some of them, if not most of them.

"Even on your best days," Tiger Woods often says, "you never make all your putts."

ON A HOT AFTERNOON IN FORT WORTH, TEXAS, A mother was helping her six-year-old son pitch and putt on a par-3 golf course when an elderly man approached them.

"Young lady," the elderly man said, "I wish to compliment you for taking the time to teach your son golf. You will never regret this effort. Your son will learn a game he can enjoy the rest of his life."

The elderly man was Ben Hogan, once the dominant golfer of his era, and in those thoughtful words to a mother and son he didn't know, he defined the essence of golf's popularity.

For anyone and everyone, golf is indeed a game to be enjoyed for a lifetime. Whether you're young or old, a man or a woman, short or tall, slim or husky, you can play golf from the time you're old enough to swing a club to the time you're too old to swing a club.

Tennis, swimming, and running are also sports for a lifetime, but golf's handicap system distinguishes it from other sports.

In golf, a handicap is measured by a person's average score, for better or for worse. For those skilled enough to average, say, par 72, their handicap would be what is known as scratch, or zero. For those who average, say, 82 or 92 or 102, their handicaps would be 10, 20, and 30, meaning their average score is that many strokes over par.

It's known as "giving" or "getting" strokes: Either the better golfer gives strokes to a lesser opponent, or the less skilled golfer gets strokes from the better opponent.

Theoretically, the handicap system places a golfer on an equal level with any other golfer—even you with Tiger Woods—either in medal play (total score) or match play (hole by hole).

Tiger Woods celebrates his hole in one at the 1996 Milwaukee Open.

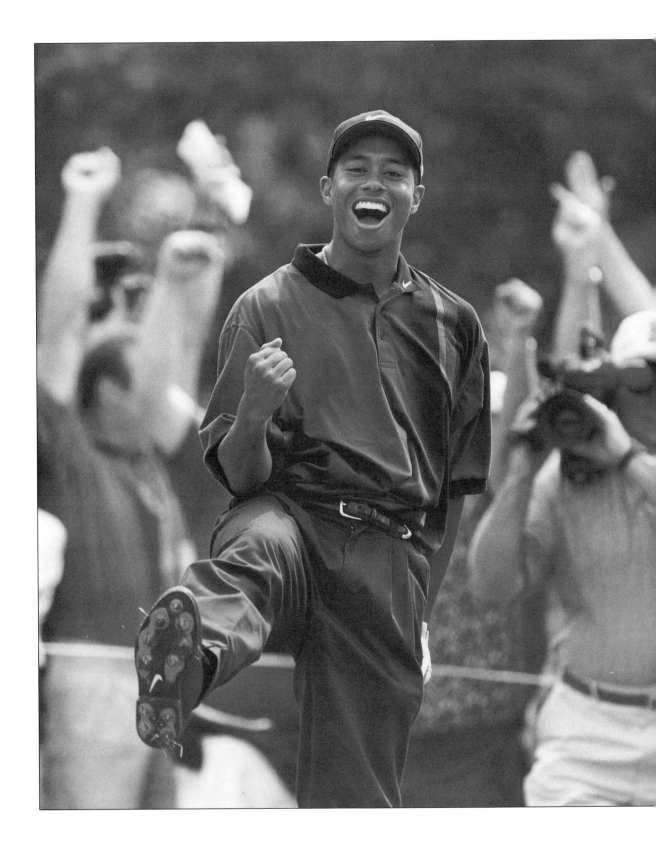

At the championship level, whether it's a national title (as conducted by the United States Golf Association) or at your local course, tournaments involve every age group from junior to senior, every gender, and sometimes both men and women in what are known as mixed events.

But golf has other elements that enhance its popularity.

No two courses are alike. For that matter, no two holes are alike. That's why golfers talk about wanting to play Pebble Beach or Pine Valley or Cypress Point or Pinehurst or Shinnecock Hills. Those and other famous courses are different from and more difficult than their home course.

When you play golf, you also surround yourself with the beauty of nature. Trees and shrubs, ponds and streams. Birds chirping. Squirrels scampering. Geese honking. Foxes running. Alligators sunning. On wilderness courses, bears and moose have often been sighted.

More than anything else, what three-time U.S. Open champion Hale Irwin once called the "onliness" of golf is part of the game's primary appeal.

Out on a golf course, you may be playing a match against someone else or with a partner, but no matter what the competitive format, it's really you against the golf course, you against par, you against yourself. Your partner can't help you hit the ball any more than your opponent can prevent you from hitting the ball.

In a game of honor and integrity, "onliness" is even more obvious. Bobby Jones and other famous players have called a penalty stroke on themselves when no one else saw the infraction. But they had seen it.

Another of golf's most appealing attributes is that no one has ever really conquered it. Bobby Jones, Ben Hogan, and Jack Nicklaus dominated the other golfers in their respective eras, but golf doesn't let anyone win every tournament. The swing is too elusive. The cup is too small.

But that is precisely why golf is so popular. It's the mountain that can't be climbed.

ace   hole in one

approach shot   stroke played with the intention of getting the ball on the green, preferably close to the hole

birdie   score of 1 below par on a hole

blade   striking area of iron club

bogey   score of 1 over par on a hole

brassie   old club equivalent to a 2-wood

bunker   depression in the ground filled with sand or grass

caddie   person engaged to carry player's clubs and offer advice if asked

chip   short, low, running shot

cup   *See* hole

dimples   indentations on the cover of a golf ball

dogleg   hole with an angled fairway

double eagle   score of 3 below par on a hole

driver   club designed to give tee shots maximum distance

eagle   score of 2 below par on a hole

fairway   mown grass between the tee and the green

Grand Slam   first used to describe Bobby Jones's 1930 winning of the Open and Amateur championships of the U.S. and Britain; now means winning the year's Masters, U.S. Open, British Open, and PGA Championship

green   area of a course prepared for putting

handicap   allowance of shots based on a golfer's average performance on a course in terms of par. *See also* stroke hole

hazard   *See* bunker; water hazard

hole   goal of the golfer; must be 4.25 inches in diameter

irons clubs with metal heads designed to provide various degrees of trajectory and distance

mashie old iron club now equivalent to a 5-iron

match play when contest is decided by whoever wins most holes

mixed event partnership of one man and one woman against another partnership of one man and one woman

muscle memory correct swing movements developed by disciplined practice

par score a golfer is expected to make at a hole; always assumes 2 putts

penalty stroke amount added to score for accidental or purposeful infringement of rules

pitch short, high shot

putter club used on the green to put ball in the hole

putting green *See* green

rough long grass on sides of fairways and greens

sand-wedge club used to get out of bunkers and sometimes off grass

scratch golfer a golfer with an average score on a course equal to the par of that course; a golfer with a zero handicap

shanks shots off the neck of the club, causing the ball to veer off sharply

spoon old club equivalent to a 3-wood

stroke intentionally hitting the ball

stroke hole where player receives or gives a stroke to his opponents under the handicap system

stroke play or **medal play** when contest is decided by total number of strokes needed to complete the course

tee area from which a golfer begins to play a hole

tee peg or **golf peg** aid on which a ball can be perched for tee shots only

water hazard any sea, lake, pond, river, creek, ditch, or other open water

wedge   club used for short, high shots or to get out of trouble spots

woods   a series of clubs, mostly made of metal now, beginning with the driver

yips or **twitch**   lack of coordination stemming from nerves that control the small muscles of the hand or wrist, usually when putting

DATE DUE

FOLLETT